'Atiyah Sa'uda Daniels

A Guide For The New Muslims Journey Towards Islam

Understanding Islamic Basics

A Guide for The new Muslims Journey Towards Islam

A Guide For The New Muslims Journey Towards Islam

Understanding Islamic Basics

'Atiyah Sauda Daniels

Contents

Contents..	2
Copyright..	4
Dedication..	5
To Allah, (s.w.t), New and Established Muslims	5
Prologue...	8
Muslim by Chance or by Choice..	8
CHAPTER ONE	24
BASIC INFORMATION ABOUT ISLAM.............................	24
CHAPTER TWO	31
CONVICTIONS IN ISLAM..	31
CHAPTER THREE...	39
WHISPERINGS FROM SHAYTAN	39
CHAPTER FOUR	46
MISCONCEPTION ABOUT ISLAM.................................	46
CHAPTER FIVE	56
THE DUTIES OF A MUSLIM...	56
CHAPTER SIX...	67
SUBMITTING ONESELF TO ALLAH	67
CHAPTER SEVEN	71

LEARNING ABOUT ISLAM	72
CHAPTER EIGHT	76
PREPARING FOR SALAT	77
CHAPTER NINE	83
PROPAGATING ISLAM	83
CHAPTER TEN	91
OBSTACLES AND CHALLENGES	91
CHAPTER ELEVEN	108
CHOICE OF FRIENDS	108
CHAPTER TWELVE	118
MAINTAINING A MODERATE PRACTICE	118
CHAPTER THIRTEEN	123
PREPARING FOR DEATH	123
CHAPTER FOURTEEN	127
THE RIGHTEOUS WALK TO ALLAH	127
CHAPTER FIFTEEN	133
SUMMARY	133
Glossary	141
REFERENCES	148

A Guide for the New Muslims Journey Towards Islam

Copyright

Copyright @ 2023 'Atiyah Sa'uda Daniels

All rights reserved. No parts of this book may be used In any manner, of any kind, without written permission except in the case of brief quotations embodied in critical articles and reviews.

ISBN-13: 979-8861199339

Amazon Kindle Direct Publishing.

Printed in the United States of America

A Guide for the New Muslims Journey Towards Islam

Dedication

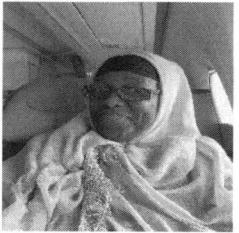

To Allah, (s.w.t), New and Established Muslims

Islam is a faith of practicality it is broad and can be viewed as a complicated Deen-ul-Fitrah (the natural faith of man), a way of life or faith.

Qur'an Surah Al-Baiyyinah: 98:[4-5])says:

"...Those who were given the Book before this (Qur'an) did not divide into sects until after there came to them a clear proof. (4) Yet, they have commanded nothing but to worship Allah, with their sincere devotion to 'Him' being True in their faith; to establish Salah (prayers); and to pay Zakah (obligatory charity), and that is the infallible true Faith."

With the blessings and assistance from Allah [s.w.t], the information within this book will have proven to be helpful and easy to understand for those individuals who have decided. to enter into the fold of Islam. The antidotal stories about the personal life of Asiah and her ex-husband Usman will give the reader an idea of some obstacles and challenges they both went through in the struggle to keep their Ibadah, (faith) as Muslims. May Allah cause your journey to be one of immense success as a 'New or existing Muslim,' Amin!

The steps to becoming a Muslim are not so hard, the individual needs to first declare, their oneness with Allah (s.w.t), by repeating these words; *(La ilaha illa-lahu Ashadu anna Muhammadan wa ashadu anna Abdulluhu wa Rasulluhu)*, meaning I bear witness that there is no deity to be worship except Allah and Muhammad is his Slave and Messenger.

The road to becoming a successful Muslim depends upon how you manage the trials and tribulations in this life, and the research one does to weed out bad Islamic information to find the truth. When you are receiving information think of what the Qur'an, the Islamic tradition, the Sunnah of the Prophet, and some authentic hadiths are guiding us in terms of how to live and behave in life.

When Asiah first accepted and entered the Deen of Islam as she was taking Shahadah, declaring her oneness to Allah (s.w.t) Asiah decided that moment to gather all the information about Islam the faith of peace. While, studying and learning in detail the actual meanings and understanding of how to practice and perform t*he required* **Five Pillars of Islam'**, *and the required* '**Articles of Faith' in Islam**. It is her understanding that every Muslim must strive to commit themselves to following these tenets of Islam for one to become a strong successful Muslim.

At the beginning of Asiah's journey towards committing herself to worshiping Allah (s.w.t), and learning how to be a practicing Muslim, there were some doubts in her mind about certain information she came across, and about the activities of some other practicing Muslims, and the things they were doing that were *'haram'*, yet they profess to be Muslim.

Asiah learned not to judge but to teach the proper type of behavior a Muslim should display by being a model Muslim and by developing her characters like that of the

Prophet (s.a.w.s) and his wives (a.s.) as it was reported by the earlier followers, Sahaabah; (Companions) of the Prophet Muhammad s.a.w.s, (Ahmed, given name by his birth mother).

In doing so Asiah has met some wonderful Muslim men and women who exhibited a natural and tranquil demeanor to the point that if they were doing some minor *'haram'* acts like smoking, drinking, or not covering up it was not for her to pass judgment, but it was her duty to model the behavior of a practicing Muslim so that one day their *'haram'* habits would change and by no means did Ashiah consider herself as a perfect Muslim. However, if others continued to witness her striving in the direction of the Qur'an and the Sunnah, perhaps some of their *'haram'* habits may eventually change because they knew better and thus wanted to behave better.

Prologue

Muslim by Chance or by Choice

Muslim by Choice: Acceptance of Islam

Once Asiah decided to accept Islam as her way of life, there were so...many stories to be told, by people who had very different views and ideas about what a Muslim should be, how they should behave, and the things one should or should not do as a Muslim. The advice given was more or less suggestive of the sunnah or traditions of Islamic teachings. With keen interest, Asiah decided to study and follow up on the *'Five Pillars Of Islam' and 'The Articles Of Faith'* as described in the Islamic doctrines.

After carefully listening to the many stories about Deen-ul Islam, she began doing some research of her own; first to find out if what was being told had any resemblance to truth and to help her develop and strengthen her path to becoming a successful strong Muslim woman. In doing so, Asiah sought the guidance of the one and only Creator Allah (s.w.t), the Almighty through Salah (prayer) and the readings of The Holy Qur'an, as well as the Holy Bible. To follow through with her research Asiah studied and learned about the different scholarly reports on the Sunnah (words and deeds of the Prophet) as well as Islamic traditions according to various Islamic scholars on the character and ways of the Prophet Muhammad s.a.w.s, (Ahmed, given birth name by his mother) written in what is known as (hadith), Asiah read and studied other scriptures like the Torah (the Five Books of Moses) sent down to the Hebrew/Israelites also known as the Twelve Tribes of Israel namely the Pharisees (Separatist) in Aramaic, and the Scribes who were also known as Pharisees. The Injeel (the 27 books of the New Testament, which includes the gospels according to Matthew, Mark, Luke, and John) which are the first four books describing the mortal life of (Isa, Ibn Maryam Jesus; a.w.s) is believed to be the one before the last prophet and messenger of the Almighty (God) and the things they say he said, and to whom the Christians say died for their sins, when in fact Isa, Ibn Maryam/Jesus; a.w.s was sent to guide the children of Israel, (Bani Isra 'il) with a book called the Injil. If this is not true, then why did he initially reject the Gentile woman looking to heal her daughter? According to the first book of the Gospel.

Matthews 15: 23-24

> (23) But he answered her not a word. And his disciples came and besought him, saying, send her away; for she cried after us. (24) But he answered and said, I am not sent but unto the lost sheep of the house of Israel."

Religion and faith are supposed to be about worshipping the Most High, (Allah, giver of life), and not (Deities and Idols). Also, for us to keep and follow the laws within the Torah. However, Muslims recognize Isa (Jesus) to be a great messenger of Allah for the salvation of humanity.

The Quran Says when the angels said,

> "O Maryam! Allah gives you the good news with a word from Him that you will be given a son; his name will be Al-Maseeh (Messiah), Isa (Jesus) the son of Maryam. He will be noble in this world and the Hereafter; and he will be from those who are very close to Allah, [45] He will speak to the people in the cradle and his maturity, and he will be among the righteous."[46]
> *(Surah A'l-e- 'Imran 3: [45-46])*

There were many more Prophets and Messengers (p.b.u.t), that Allah sent as a warning to the people of this Dunyah (world). In addition, Asiah gained her strength through prayer and surrounding myself with individuals who were practicing their Deen (way of life or faith) with the best of intentions.

There are two types of individual Muslims, they are those who were born in the Deen of Islam/way of life, and those who were chosen and accepted the Deen (way of life or Faith) of Islam. As for Asiah, she has chosen Islam because Allah (s.w.t.) has chosen to guide her to the straight path of righteousness as He, helped her to learn and understand why practicing Islam and identifying herself as a Muslim, and why Islam is the right way to live. As Asiah began to walk this road as a practicing Muslim, she also found a greater sense of peace.

Asiah did not draft this book to bash the faiths of anyone else, however, she has been blessed to experience living and practicing two distinct types of religious faiths. The first was learning about Christianity from her parents and her pastor. When she was a young child, Asiah, and her siblings were raised in a Christian home where they learned Christian values and a variety of life lessons. Asiah's parents stressed the need to respect the beliefs of others more than any other lesson.

Being born into the faith of Christianity as a (Baptist) gave her a lot of insight into the various Church organizations and how their members worshiped. Some Churches were subtle, quiet, and reserved, there weren't any replications of what they call Saints.

There were no statuses of Isa (Jesus) or his mother (Maryam) in the Churches she grew up attending, Asiah had no problem with attending church services with family, except when the Easter holiday came around. Each year her family would attend Churches that were loud praising and screaming the name of Isa (Jesus), who by the way is not the son of Allah (s.w.t) the Most High as most Christians believe him to be, Isa (Jesus), is the son of Maryam, and the divine messenger of Allah who was sent as a guide with a revelation for the Children of Bani Israel, who rejected him. Asiah's family attended the more sanctified holy ghost shouting types of Churches, which caused fear in her spirit instead of peace and calm so much so that Asiah requested her mother to please not force her to attend those types of churches again with their many different replications of deceased Biblical people of the Books the (Torah and Gospel), that were being displayed on the walls and around the Church buildings as the members called upon these statuses for help in this life, just did not make any sense to her when the Books (Torah, Gospel and The Qur'an) teaches otherwise.

In the Qur'an, Allah speaks to (the Jews and the Christians).

"O People of the Book! Do not transgress the limits of your faith. Speak nothing but the Truth about Allah. The Messiah, Isa (Jesus), the son of Maryam (Mary) was no more than a Rasool of Allah and His Word "Be" which He bestowed on Maryam and a Spirit from Him. So, believe in Allah and His Rasools and do not say: Trinity (three)." Stop saying that it is better for you Allah is only one Deity. He is far above the need to have a son! To Him belongs all that is in the heavens and the earth. Allah is All-Sufficient as a Disposer of affairs." [171] ***(Surah An-Nisa: 4[171])***

As Asiah continued with her readings of the Holy Bible, in comparison with the Noble Holy Qur'an some information did not match up with what the Church Ministers were preaching.

As she was moving away from the Church at the tender age of fifteen years, it was at that moment she truly became aware of the differences in the teachings of individual Scholars, Ministers, and Imam as Asiah began her journey towards Islam to understand the basics of its teachings. After several months of reading Islamic Books, researching, and making comparisons of the information given to her by others, she concluded this Deen (way of life) its Sunnah, and Islamic tradition by doing a detailed analysis and comparison of the three most popular faiths Islam, Judaism and Christianity.

Islam, Judaism, and Christianity are more alike in terms of the Messengers and Prophets who were chosen by Allah to deliver laws, commandments, and guidance to the people of the Books (Jews and Christians) and then the Quran through Prophet Muhammad (s.a.w.s) as a guide with a new revelation to all of mankind as a final confirmation of the Torah (Laws) through Musa/Moses and Injeel (Warning's) through Isa/Jesus from Allah to those who were not following 'His' words (kalimatu). It had been revealed to her from the signs of Allah (s.w.t), through the teachings and readings of all 'His' scriptures, Asiah understood that the people of the Books, Torah (Musa/Moses), Injeel Gospel (Isa/Jesus), Zuboor (Daud/David), and the Qur'an, Prophet Muhammad, a.w.s (Ahmed birth name given by his mother), were followers of 'The one true (illah) God' (Allah s.w.t) (peace and blessings upon them all). Islam had the most value of peace, for her in this life. Islam gave a sense of calm to Asiah's spirit and her burdens felt lighter, Islam taught her how to meditate and to control the anger within. However, being a woman of emotions, it has been difficult many a day to control that anger so when she felt the anger coming on, she grabbed the Qur'an and began praying asking Allah, (s.w.t) for His guidance with some prayers she had memorized. You see in Islam being a practicing Muslim is not about praising another human being, or praising and worshiping any status of Saint's, Prophets, or Messengers. It is about the practicing of the _Five Pillars"_ and the pure understanding and honest belief in all that the _'Articles of Faith'_ represent in Islam. As Muslims, we say _'Alhamdulillah'_ (All praise is due to Allah), and we say *'Salla-Allahu 'Alayhi wa Sallam'* (Blessings of Allah and Peace be upon him.) when we mention the name of the Prophet Muhammad, s.a.w.s. (Ahmed, his birth name given by his mother) and for all other Prophets, we ask that Allah (s.w.t) bestow His blessings and peace upon them *(alayhi wa salaam)* as He, Allah, (s.w.t) may also be pleased with them.

Islam Faith of Peace

IS Islam truly a Faith of Peace? Well from the research and studies of the Holy Qur'an and the Holy Bible after thoroughly comparing them both Asiah has found so many similarities that it motivated her towards becoming a Muslim, and in answer to her question of Islam being a faith of peace, yes, it is! Even though there are talks of wars, fighting, and dispute within the Qur'an, she still found Through reading and further research Asiah learned that the very word 'Peace' is absolutely one of Allah's attributes that explains how He (Allah), is the authority of such peace, (As-Salam) meaning *'The Peace.'* While Islam, Judaism, and Christianity all have a history of fighting for the freedom of the oppressed and the right to keep their properties. It took some time before Allah (s.w.t) gave the Prophet Muhammad, s.a.w.s. (Ahmed, given birth name by his mother) permission to go to war with his oppressors Allah, (s.w.t) first instructed the Prophet to strike a contractual agreement with the Quraish Tribe, the desert Arabs, (Bedouins), and the Jews but they broke that treaty with the murders of innocent Muslim men, and women. Even at the end of these wars the Prophet Muhammad, s.a.w.s. *(Ahmed, given birth name by his mother)* spared the lives of his captives and set free anyone who would teach the Muslims how to read and write. Many of the captives accepted Islam as their new Deen (way of life or Faith) without being forced, you see there is no compulsion to accept Islam as your faith. it was the model character of the Prophet (s.a.w.s) and his nobility that called others to accept Islam as their Deen (way of life or Faith), he was known as the trustworthy (Sadiq). From experience and through research Muslims who have chosen Islam as Allah chose them. Struggle to continue the straight and righteous path while studying the true Deen (way of life or faith) as they continue to learn the original language of the Qur'an, (Arabia) and commit themselves to Salah (prayer), they are happy and excited about being a Muslim and practicing their Deen (way of life or faith) Islam. The Deen of Islam has given Asiah great joy and solace it helped her to cope with the pitfalls of life and even still she is excited to identify herself as a Muslim walking towards the roads of Islamic success. Many Muslims who were born into Islam take the Deen for granted because they feel a sense of entitlement.

They were taught from childhood how to memorize and read the Qur'an in Arabic with whatever cultural and local language translation that can give meaning to the Arabic Qur'an, since Allah revealed the Qur'an in the language of the Arabs (Arabic) for them to understand, even still the Qur'an was sent for all of mankind, and it was years before the development and printing of Quranic Arabic by Paganino and his son Alessandro Paganini according to historians between 1537 and 1538. There was a great need for the printing of the Qur'an because the companions of the Prophet, Muhammad (s.a.w.s), and several Muslims who memorized the Qur'an were dying especially during the time of war which ignited the urgency for compiling the surahs and ayahs of the Qur'an in book form.

However, those Muslims who have chosen Islam for the love of Allah, (s.w.t) His guidance and instruction written in the Qur'an their path to righteousness have a stronger commitment than most that are Muslim by chance (birth) because they are proud to be identified as a practicing Muslim. Not to say that those born into Islam through their Muslim father and mother are not proud because they are it is the pressures of being raised as a Muslim and then having to blend in with non-Muslims who don't wish to learn about our Deen (way of life or faith). Asiah is speaking from the experience of her children who are Muslims by chance (birth). They shy away from being identified as

Muslim because of the state of the world today, how people are frowning down on Muslims and attacking them for being Muslims. Asiah's children had to go through these same types of harassment during the late 70s and early 80s up until their adult lives. They are holding on to the knowledge of Islam as they teach it to others who ask. One thing is for sure Asiah said, she will continue to be a practicing Muslim regardless of what others may think or feel about Islam being this faith that preaches nothing but hate which is far from the truth. The Quran teaches that we must find commonalities and walk away from any arguments about our revelations.

Allah (s.w.t) says in The Qur'an.

> "When you see those who are engaged in arguments about our revelations, turn away from them until they change their topic of discussion. If Shaitan ever makes you forget this commandment, then as soon as you realize, withdraw from the company of wrongdoers." [68] ***(Surah Al-An'am: 6[68])***

Asiah learned It was not an easy task keeping her children under the security of Islam for various reasons e.g., living among non-Muslims who teased and made fun of the children and of herself for dressing against what they viewed as the norm of society, having to send her children to schools that were not Islamic schools with educator who were as bad as the students in disrespecting our faith. This caused great mental harm and uneasiness for the children, what a society we live in where religious tolerance for Islam was not quite there yet and still has some ways to go.

Asiah and her children had two strikes against them while living here in America and the children were born of a dark hue *(Black)* and born into the deen of Islam as Muslims. The Qur'an teaches to the whole of humanity in this society, Allah (s.w.t) did not just send revelations to the Prophet Muhammad s.a.w.s *(Ahmed, given birth name by his mother)* on how to teach the Arab Nations about Islam and how to become practicing Muslims. Allah *(s.w.t)* also sent the Qur'an as a reminder of the Prophets and Messengers who are known as the 'People of the Books'(Torah and Gospel) explaining the behavior, practices, and characteristics of the believers and the unbelievers. Making the Qur'an a guide for all of humanity and a conformational seal of all scriptures, Prophets, and Messengers with Muhammad, s.a.w.s (Ahmed, given birth name by his mother) being the last and final Prophet and Messenger sent by Allah (s.w.t) once again as a warning to Mankind.

Born into Islam: Muslim by Chance

Ex-husband, Usman, who was born in the Country Nigeria, in the Continent of Africa into Deen-ul Islam, as a Muslim explained his own story about his journey through Deen-ul Islam (way of life or faith) and why he chooses to continue being a practicing Muslim of Islam. He is Muslim by Chance *(birth)* because his parents are Muslim while my parents are Christians with an understanding of Islam. So, if you feel being Muslim by choice is a bit difficult then you should hear the story of someone who is Muslim by chance meaning from birth. Usman who was, born into Islam, tells me two stories about his journey as a 'New Muslim.' Now just because he was born into the faith of Islam does not make him automatically understand all the dos and don'ts of practicing Islam and being a good Muslim.

He grew up in his home with both his mother and father who are Muslim but still learning about the Deen of Islam, its practices, and what they should, and should not do as Muslims. Usman recalled a story about when he was attending Secondary High School in Nigeria, he would not go outside the house without putting on his (Kufis,) type of men's head covering for Muslims. His father would tease him about always wearing a (Kufis/Tahj) his father informed his son Usman that he didn't need to cover his head all the time, as this was the information received from his father which he paid close attention, keep in mind there is no compulsion in Islam it is said to be the Sunnah of Prophet, Muhammad s.a.w.s (Ahmed, given birth name by his mother) who according to hadith's wore a turban which is a head covering worn in different ways and called by different names depending on the region and culture. It is Mustahabb (a beloved thing) according to hadith's, (Sahih Muslim, vol. 2 book of Hajj number 3148). We as Muslims need to first research any information given to us so that we may practice our Deen (way of life or faith) correctly and not take things at face value no matter where the information is being obtained. It was narrated from Anas bin Malik that the Messenger of Allah (s.w.t.) said:

(Sunan Ibn Majah, Vol. 1, Book 1, Hadith 224)

> "Seeking knowledge is a duty upon every Muslim, and he who imparts knowledge to those who do not deserve it is like one who puts a necklace of jewels, pearls, and gold around the neck of swine.'

If Usman, Asiah's ex-husband, and his father had remembered the above Hadith, they would have remembered to seek knowledge about such an issue of men not having to cover their heads like that of the Muslim women. Then possibly they both could have come to a sound agreed-upon consensus that the wearing of a (Kufis/Tahj) for Muslim men was a part of the dress code and not as he had been taught that Muslim men didn't need to cover their head as that of the Muslim Women. How else can you identify as being a Muslim other than telling someone that you are a Muslim and the way that both men and women of Islam dress in society? Usman eventually stopped donning his Kufis or Tahj daily after learning that it was not a common habit among most Muslim males in his country. After all, his father was the one who first made Usman aware that wearing a Kufi or Tahj every day was not necessary for Muslim men, at least not until he noticed a change in the way his son was still dressing in his Jalabiya or thobe (traditional attire for Muslim men), but without a head covering.

Usman's father now started to enquire as to why his son had suddenly changed the way he dressed. This question was raised when his father's independent investigation revealed that wearing a (Kufis/Tahj) style head covering for males in Islam was a good and noble deed in one's faith. As you can see, even our parents who are born into Islam don't always understand all there is to know about being a practicing Muslim and the revelations within the Qur'an on dress codes and behaviors of a believing Muslim.

Allah has sent the Qur'an as a guide for all of mankind, to be delivered by the Prophet Muhammad s.a.w.s *(Ahmed, given name by his mother)*. If we, as parents who identify as Muslim, don't take the time to research and learn the truth about what is Sunnah or traditional in Islam, we run the risk of misinforming others and giving the wrong impression to our children or even other Muslims, both practicing and non-practicing. The Hadith by _(Sahih Bukhari)_ quotes the Prophet Muhammad s.a.w.s. *(Ahmed; his mother gave him this birth name)* as stated, _"Seeking knowledge is the duty of every Muslim."_ This is because knowledge is power. We shouldn't rush to pass judgment on people who live by the Traditions and Sunnah of Prophet Muhammad s.a.w.s. *(Ahmed, given birth name by his mother)*, until Muslim parents take the time to learn for themselves what are the Traditional and Sunnah ways of dressing according to the Qur'an and authentic Hadiths, we run the risk of misinforming others who would like to understand our Islamic faith. Similar considerations apply to non-Muslim parents who discover that their child has chosen Islam as their Deen (way of life or faith). Understand that knowledge is a responsibility and an honorable task of every Muslim and that wearing Islamic clothing should become a goal for every believing practicing Muslim to help identify oneself as a Muslim. According to the Qur'an, it states, anyone among His followers who gets knowledge is in fear (Taqwa) of Him (Allah).

Surah Fatir: 35: [28])

"...In fact, only those among His servants who possess knowledge fear Allah; surely, Allah is All-Mighty, All-Forgiving," (28)

Because they understand the true powers and blessing of Allah, the one who can destroy humanity and replace humankind with a new set of human beings. Has the Most High (God) in our past not destroyed Sodom and Gomar? And cause a great flood during the error of Noah and the Ark Therefore, seek knowledge until the day Allah calls you to your death.

In the Qur'an Allah (s.w.t) asked.

"Have these people not learned a lesson that 'We' have destroyed before them many generations in whose ruins they walk through? Certainly, in these ruins, there are signs for people to understand. (128) (Surah Ta-Ha: 20: [128])

The people of understanding are those who have studied and obtained the true knowledge of Islam, the Qur'an, and the Sunnah traditions and behaviors of the Prophet Muhammad s.a.w.s (Ahmed, given birth name by his mother), as he displayed such behaviors and mannerisms that caused the worst of mankind to become noble men and women all because the Prophet exuded the characters of (Sadiq) and (Salam) a man who was trustworthy and peaceful. Again, in Islam, a Muslim learns from the cradle to the grave. Then Usman told his ex-wife Asiah another tale about going to college and joining an Islamic group that taught and spoke about basic features and difficulties in Islam, as well as what it meant to be a practicing Muslim. Usman made it a habit to attend these lectures at least once a week. However, his dedication to these lectures posed a problem when he would return home late, prompting his father to lock him out. His father, concerned about Usman's late-night activities, wanted to know where he was returning from at that late hour. It wasn't until later that the father discovered Usman was visiting an Islamic organization to study and listen to lectures.

Upon learning about his son's activities, Usman's father decided to forbid him from joining such an organization in the future, as he saw such Islamic meetings as fanatical, until one day the same organization that his father regarded as fanatical built a massive Masjid in Nigeria's Islamic community in the neighborhood where Usman's family lived. As Asiah's father-in-law began to attend the new Masjid, he listened to the khutbah (Sermon) speech that his son received from the same Islamic group that my father-in-law earlier said his son was listening to extremists. He made these comments before he realized what the Islamic organization was about.

The Khutbah (Sermon) was essential in changing his opinion of the Islamic organization in his area, soon the eyes and heart of my father-in-law were now beginning to reopen as he embraced and received the new information. This is why no one should be quick to prejudge something or someone before they have an opportunity to gain experience and study more about people, places, and things. There are so many people within society that have a misconception about the true worshiping Muslims and the Deen of Islam which provokes fear into their minds and hearts only because they have no real knowledge of our practices and the ways we live in peace only what mass Media Television is showing them about the atrocities being committed by terrorist who say they are Muslims while causing the deaths of innocent men, women and children who are Muslim and non-Muslim alike. Asiah's father-in-law was now requesting that his son join such an Islamic organization to become a prestigious member of the Islamic community, so once again my father-in-law by the guidance of Allah (s.w.t) was given further indication that the direction his son was heading in, was bringing him closer to Allah, (s.w.t) and teaching him how to maintain his righteous walk as a Muslim. The father realizes he should have offered encouragement instead of discouraging his son. He acknowledges that he should have taken the time to research the Islamic organization that his son is involved with before jumping to conclusions. This way, he would have had a better understanding of the group and could have provided more informed support for his son. Knowledge, tolerance, patience, and respect are the lessons imparted to both father and son in these examples.

As children, we wish for our parents to be proud that we are following in the footsteps of our righteous parents but as we become older, we still look for guidance from our parents even though we wish to fly our wings in life. Remember, to always continue respecting the ideals and advice from your parents unless it clashes with Allah's instructions and guidance within the Qur'an as given to the Prophet Muhammad, a.w.s (Ahmed, given birth name by his mother).

The Qur'an says, The Bedouins (The Arabs') said.

"We have believed." Tell them: "You have not believed; rather say "we have become Muslims;' for faith has not yet found its way into your hearts. If you obey Allah and His Rasool, He will not deny you the reward of your deeds; surely, Allah is Forgiving, Merciful." [14] (Surah Al-Hujurat: 49: [14])

Asiah selected this particular verse because it sheds light on the concept that verbal declarations of faith do not always reflect the true state of our hearts. It highlights the importance of aligning our words with our internal beliefs and values, emphasizing the significance of genuine faith and devotion beyond mere verbal expression. Being known as a Muslim says that I will continue to strive towards becoming one who receives Islam in my heart, and soul, not just the mere utterance of words telling everyone that I am a believer of Islam. Because one thing is for sure, Allah, (s.w.t) knows our true hearts and thoughts and sometimes we have doubts. Therefore, as Muslim parents, we need to be up on our current studies about the Qur'an, the Sunnah, and current world events so that we can become better Islamic guides to our children, families, and those seeking information about the practice of Islam. Whether you are Muslim by Chance (*birth*) or Choice (*acceptance*) it does not necessarily mean that you receive an automatic pass, we would still be considered as a 'New Muslim' striving towards righteousness just as I am even though I have been practicing Islam for more than thirty (30 years) I still don't know everything there is to learn and understand about Deen-ul Islam. There were some things Usman's father had not taken a closer look at and it caused him to misinform his son and tease him about it. For instance, wearing his Taj daily and attending Islamic gatherings would deepen his understanding, and knowledge about the Deen (way of life or faith) and how to become a successful practicing Muslim. So, as you can see, whether by choice (acceptance) or by chance (birth), we are all still "New Muslims" because the learning never stops until we are in our graves. As you pursue knowledge, it is crucial to diligently verify the credibility and accuracy of the information presented, whether it is through spoken word, reported news, or written content. There is a Hadith according to (Sahih Muslim) that reported The Prophet (s.a.w.s.) said: "Whoever seeks a way to acquire knowledge Allah will make easy his way to Paradise." [p. 2699] Then there is an ayah in Qur'an that Allah, (Ta'ala) said to The Prophet Muhammad, s.a.w.s.(Ahmed, his given name by his mother); about being in a hurry to recite the Qur'an before its completion, as he tells him to ask for an increase in his knowledge.

(Ta-Ha: 20[114])

"High and exalted be Allah, the True King! Do not hasten to recite the Qur'an before its revelation is completely conveyed to you and say: "O my Rabb! Increase my knowledge. [114 p.434]

As Allah has revealed in this ayah to the Prophet Muhammad s.a.w.s (*Ahmed, given name by his mother*) advising him not to hasten to give a recitation of the Qur'an before completion, this is the same way we as Muslims should handle the way we convey information to others, and this includes our children, by ensuring that we have completed all the research required to confirm the authenticity of the information given. Don't forget to always ask Allah (s.w.t) for help in increasing your knowledge as you continue to study up until the day of your death.

Remember <u>Sahih Muslim</u>, reported the Prophet Muhammad s.a.w.s (*Ahmed, given name by his mother*) as saying.

Sahih Muslim (Hadith)

"Whoever seeks a way to acquire knowledge Allah will make easy his way to Paradise." **(p. 2699) Amin!**

CHAPTER ONE

BASIC INFORMATION ABOUT ISLAM

Quranic Juz (part) – 4 Surah (A'l-e- 'Imran: 3: (104-105); pg. 172. States as follows:

"Let there arise from among you a band of people who should invite to righteousness, enjoin good and forbid evil; such are the ones, who shall be successful." (104)

"Be not like those, who became divided into sects and who started to argue against each other after clear revelations had come to them. Those responsible for division and arguments will be sternly punished." (105)

Throughout my journey in the search for the truth about the proper ways to practice Islam, there is one major instruction from Allah (s.w.t) that I am constantly working on and that is helping people to understand that there is only one Islam and there should be no division among those who call themselves Muslim.

Allah clearly said in the Qur'an for us to "be not like those, who became divided into sects." *(Surah 'A-e-'Imran: 3:105)* because doing so will for sure cause arguments among the believing Muslims fighting to prove which tribe (sect) of Islam is truly living in the way of the Qur'an as instructed by Allah, (s.w.t) and the Sunnah, as demonstrated, and taught by the Prophet Muhammad s.a.w.s (*Ahmed, given name by his mother*). Therefore, I have decided not to claim an Islamic denomination when it comes to practicing my faith Islam, I am just known as a Muslima and the Qurán says if they ask you who you are tell them you are Muslim. We are all one brother and one sister under the tenets of Islam, as we declare ourselves to be Muslims. Please remember the text below:

As Allah has instructed, and as demonstrated by the Prophet Muhammad (s.a.w.s) (Ahmed, given name by his mother) to the earlier Companions (Sahaabahs) and followers of Islam, it is reported that, according to the Hadiths by Bukhari and Muslim, and Riyadus Saliheen (a compilation of Hadiths), the Prophet Muhammad (s.a.w.s.) did not turn anyone away, whether they were Jew, Christian, or someone with no faith. He was there to help and to make peace among them. Muslims must strive to acquire the same characteristics as those of the Prophet (s.a.w.s). He was known as Sadiq, which means "a person who is very upright and true," a character type that all Muslims should strive to embody.

The Qur'an explains the meaning of Righteousness as Qur'an Al-Baqarah: 2[177]

"Righteousness is not whether you turn your face towards East or West, but righteousness is to believe in Allah, the Last Day, the Angels, the Books, and the Prophets, to spend wealth despite love for it. On relatives, orphans, helpless, needy travelers, those who ask for and on the redemption of captives; to establish Salah (prayers), to pay Zakah (charity), to fulfill promises when made, to be steadfast in poverty, hardship and at the time of war. Those are the ones who are truthful, and those are the ones who are pious. (177)

First, as individuals, we need to understand that there are several types of Muslims. However, the Holy Qur'an teaches us there is only one Islam with 'Five obligatory Pillars' and 'The Articles of Faith' which every Muslim must follow and agree to, and they are.

The Pillars of Islam:

I. <u>Tawheed (Oneness in Allah)</u>: La illah ill Allah; There is no (Creator) God but He, Surah Ali-Imran.

II. <u>Salat</u> (Obligatory Prayers): prescribed Five times daily.

III. <u>Zakhat</u> (Obligatory Charity): (10%) or the least amount of (2.5%) of your annual salary, charitable deeds to others, or <u>Sadaqah</u> (Optional) Charitable giving is seen as a lovely loan to Allah. Includes lending a hand to those in need or simply smiling at someone to make their day.

IV. <u>Sawm / Ramadan (Fasting)</u>: All those who profess to be Muslim must fast for thirty days during the Holy month of Ramadan.

V. <u>Hajj (Pilgrimage)</u>: Every Muslim should prepare for their journey to Makkah at least once in their lifetime if they are financially able to do so.

The Articles of Faith:

"To believe in Allah, His angels, His Scriptures, His Rasool's, The Day of Resurrection, and to believe in the Divine Decree (Al-Qadar), both its Good and Evil." *(Reported by Bukhari and Muslim)*

I. *Allah:* Belief and conviction in the existence of Allah and His Oneness (Tawheed). Tawheed is divided into three categories to facilitate its understanding:

a) *Taheed Al-Rububiyah:* (The Unity of His Lordship): To believe that Allah Alon is the Rabb of this universe. (The Institute of Islamic Knowledge, 1997, p. 94).

b) *Tawheed Al-Uluhiyah:* (The Unity of His Worship): To believe that Allah is the only ' llah (God, object of adoration and worship). (The Institute of Islamic Knowledge, 1997, p. 94).

c) *Tawheed Al-Asma wa As-Sifat:* (The Unity of His Names and Attributes): "To believe in all of Allah's names and attributes in their perfect, absolute forms." (The Institute of Islamic Knowledge, 1997, p. 94).

II. *His Angels:* To believe in the presence of angels, their names, traits, and functions as detailed in the Qur'an and reliable Prophetic tradition and Sunnah (peace be upon him)." (The Institute of Islamic Knowledge, 1997, p. 94).

III. *His Books:* "To have faith in Allah's Book of Revelations as compassion and guidance to His diverse Rasool's.

- *Tawrat (Torah) revealed to Musa (Moses),*
- *The Injeel (Gospel) revealed to 'Isa (Jesus),*
- *The Zuboor (Psalm) revealed to Daud (David and.*
- *The Qur'an revealed to Muhammad, (Ahmed, peace be upon them all.)"*

IV. His Rasool's (Messengers): "To have faith in all of the Prophets listed in the Qur'an and that Allah sent a Messenger to every group of people." (The Institute of Islamic Knowledge, 1997, p. 94).

V. The Last Day (the hereafter): "To believe in everything the Prophet, peace be upon him, or the Qur'an have mentioned regarding the last hour." (The Institute of Islamic Knowledge, 1997, p. 94).

VI. <u>The Belief in the divine Decree (Al-Qadar), both, the Good, and the Evil thereof:</u> To have the conviction that Allah knew things before they were. Therefore, everything concerning His creation's obedience, disobedience, lifespans, and nourishment is contained in this earth. (The Institute of Islamic Knowledge, 1997, p. 94).

Therefore, in essence *'The Five Pillars of Islam'* and 'The <u>'Articles of Faith,'</u> are truly summed up in The Holy Qur'an the Surah of *(Al-Ahzab: 33 ayahs 35-36)* states, in paraphrase summary,

Surah (Al-Ahzab: 33 ayahs 35-36)

"Surely, the Muslim men and the Muslim women, the believing men and women, the devout men and women, the truthful men and women, the patient men and women, the humble men and women, the charitable men and women, the fasting men and women, the men and the women who guard their chastity, and the men and the women who remember Allah much – for all of them, Allah has prepared forgiveness and a great reward." (35)

"It is not fitting for a believing man or believing woman to have an option in their affairs when a matter has been decided by Allah His Rasool, and whoever disobeys Allah and His Rasool has indeed strayed *into a clearly wrong path."* (36) **(Al-Ahzab: 33 ayahs 35-36)**

Considering this, if you are a believer male or female and you confess your sins and give thanks to Allah, "He" has already pardoned you, and those who believe will receive a great reward because Allah undoubtedly keeps his word when it comes to preparing forgiveness and a great reward these same words are found throughout the Holy Qur'an.

As you shall discover, Allah (s.w.t) is not a deceiver of Mankind but Shaitan (c.h.) is the one who deceives at any cause, he tells you so in the Qur'an and the Bible. Islam is not about blind faith it is about understanding what is right and wrong by doing a true comparison of what happened when the 'People of the Book' (Jews and Christians) disobeyed the guidance and commandments of Allah and what happened when the Tribe of Quraish people (Bedouins) Arabs disobeyed the guidance and commandments of Allah. As a 'New Muslim you must strive hard to stay on the straight path of righteousness and to continue seeking the true knowledge of Islam, and that you lead by being a model Muslim for the sake of Allah. You don't walk blindly into the Deen or Faith of Islam but do your research in seeking out the truth from the past of the pre-Islamic error and notice how Allah made once limitless things have limits such; as the number of wives one man can have, and to abstain from drinking intoxicants, and the duration that one must fast. The events were unfolding which led people to follow the Prophet Muhammad s.a.w.s (Ahmed, given name by his mother). Learn to see how what was once permitted has been deemed unlawful and how the treatment of a group (slaves, the impoverished, and women) has been accorded rights. You will be tasked with proving to others that we are peaceful Muslims once you have a firm grip on the ***"Five Pillars" and the "Articles of Faith."*** The more knowledge you seek about your Deen the closer you get to Allah (s.w.t), and the traditions and characteristics of the Prophet Muhammad s.a.w.s (*Ahmed, given name by his mother*). People who do not seek knowledge to comprehend the commands that Allah gives to mankind will never be on par with those who have discovered the knowledge they seek in the understanding of the Qur'an and the Sunnah because those who know will always be one step ahead of those who do not.

(Qur'an Surah Az-Zumar: 39 [9] Allah (s.w.t) said,

> "Can he who is obedient, pass the hours of night prostrating in worship or standing in adoration, fearing the hereafter, and hoping to earn the Mercy of his Rabb, be compared to the man who does not? Are those who know equal to those who do not know? None will take heed except the people of understanding." [9] **(Qur'an Surah Az-Zumar: 39 [9]**

According to Islamic scholars, when a Muslim stands in Tahjud prayer, it is a voluntary prayer that can be offered or fulfilled before Fajr. Tahjud is a prayer in which Allah decides who will respond to it, hence it is only by invitation from Allah. Whether it is two, four, six, or eight rakats, you must understand that Allah has selected you, and sometimes Allah invites you through a challenge he places in your life. (Mufti Ismail ibn Musa Menk)

CHAPTER TWO

CONVICTIONS IN ISLAM

The Qur'an is guidance for the whole of creation sent by Allah (s.w.t) through his Prophet Muhammad s.a.w.s (*Ahmed, given name by his mother*), as we declare our oneness to Allah (s.w.t), (La illaha illallah wa Muhammadan Rasool Allah).

(Surah A'l-e-'Iman: 3 [1-6]: pg. 160)

"Allah, There is no 'God' but He, the Living, the Eternal. [2] He has revealed to you this Book with the Truth, confirming the scripture which preceded it, as He revealed the Tawrat (Torah) and Injeel (Gospel),[3] before this, as a guidance for mankind and also revealed this Al-Furqan (criterion for judgment between right and wrong). Surely, those who reject Allah's revelations will be sternly punished; Allah is Mighty, and capable of retribution. [4] (**Surah A'l-e-'Iman: 3 [1-6]: pg. 160**)

The word conviction in the legal circle has been defined to mean a sentencing or judgment of someone charged with a crime and the outcome is a conviction.

This very same word also means one who has a firmly held belief or opinion, (view, thought, persuasion, idea position, or stance). *'Conviction'* is something certain; a judgment of guilt in court and a *'Strong Belief'* are both convictions. Prosecutors file motions to charge a defendant with a crime, by producing evidence for a guilty verdict, in legal terms is a conviction. Then you have defense attorneys who present evidence for a non-guilty verdict to prevent a conviction.

The same word conviction is also a set of beliefs and principles, like those of *'The Five Pillars of Islam' and 'The Articles of Faith,'* which the practicing Muslims should adhere to. In Islam, the Articles of Faith are the fundamental beliefs that every Muslim should uphold. These include belief in Allah, the angels, the revealed books, the prophets, the Day of Judgment, and divine predestination. The Five Pillars of Islam are the core acts of worship that every Muslim must adhere to, including the declaration of faith, prayer, fasting during the calendar month of Ramadan, almsgiving, and the pilgrimage to Mecca for those who are able. These beliefs and practices form the foundation of Islamic conviction and are integral to the faith of every Muslim. We are required to perform Salah (prayer) Five times daily and participate in Zakat (Charity) and Ramadan (Fasting), annually during a lunar calendar year.

The performance of Haj (when affordable) should be attempted by all Muslims. However, Salah (prayer) and Zakah (Charity) are the two most important Pillars of Islam; and I am not saying that the other pillars are any less important. It is our duty as Muslims, to establish our conviction in the practice of these Islamic five pillars for Allah to be pleased with us. As Muslims, we give Sadaqat (Voluntary charity) and Zakah, (Obligatory charity) the difference between the two is that zakah is subjected to the conditions that one full Hijri (year) has passed since acquiring the wealth and that the wealth meets the minimum threshold (nisaab) and it is a specific portion of wealth (2.5%). Sure, here's the rewritten text: Sadaqat is not subjected to any conditions and may be given at any time, in any amount. Zakah and Sadaqah both mean worshipping Allah by giving money or various kinds of charity, no matter how small, even just a smile. All of this is done to help the needy, the poor, or those who have committed to serving Allah.

'It is revealed in the Qur'an that Allah (Ta'ala) said.
(Surah At-Tauba: 9[60])

> (60) "Zakah expenditures are only for the poor and for the needy and for those employed to collect [zakah] and for bringing hearts together [for Islam] and for freeing captives [or slaves] and for those in debt and for the cause of Allah and for the [stranded] traveler- an obligation [imposed] by Allah. And Allah is Knowing and Wise."

As you can read in the above Surah Allah specifically stated that Zakah be given to certain types of people and not to anyone else. Allah has also described those in charge of administering the funds. This is designed to bring people to the truth and to help those in need. Salah (prayer), for Muslims, is a great deal because we perform this particular Pillar of Islam to worship Allah and to ask that 'He, grant us his forgiveness of our sins and ask that he accept our prayers for ourselves, our family, friends, and most of all that Allah (s.w.t) help and protect us against the unbelievers, as we are striving to be better Muslims towards the path of righteousness of which he has decreed for all Mankind.

t states in Qur'an. (Al-Baqarah: 2: [286])

> (286) "…Our Rabb! Lay not on us the kind of burden that we have no strength to bear. Pardon us, forgive us, have mercy on us. You are our Protector, help us against the unbelievers."

There are three major duties of every Muslim they are (1) Learning about Islam, (2) Practicing Islam, and (3) Teaching people about Islam. This chapter will focus on how to practice while strengthening our convictions in **_The Pillars of Islam' and 'The Articles of Faith._** '*Allah* created humanity with different capabilities of which he knows our limitations. Allah never places a burden upon us that is beyond our capacity to bear.

[Quran Al-Baqarah: 2:286]

> (286) "Allah does not burden any human being with more than he can bear. Everyone will enjoy the credit of his deeds and suffer the debits of his wrongdoings. The believers say, "Our Rabb! Do not punish us if we forget or make a mistake. Our Rabb! Do not place on us a burden as you placed on those before us."

Take for example; Salah (prayer) if you are sick and cannot stand up for prayer you are allowed to sit down and perform your Salah. If sitting down is also an inconvenience for you then you can lay down to make Salah. Even if the use of water has become an issue for you then it is acceptable for you to use the sand of the earth for your ablution Allah (s.w.t) has made Salah very simplified for Muslims.

(Qur'an Al-e-Imran 3: 190-191)

> Allah says, (190) "In the creation of the heavens and the earth, and the alternation of night and day, there are signs for people of Intelligence." (191) "Those who remember Allah while standing, sitting, and lying on their sides and give thought to the creation of the heavens and the earth, [saying], "Our Lord You did not create this aimlessly; exalted are You [above such a thing]; then protect us from the punishment of the Fire."

Fasting in Islam is compulsory for every adult Muslim. Yet there are those Muslims who by Allah's Mercy are exempt from fasting, those that are sick, traveling long distances or breastfeeding, and Menstruating women.

Kalimatu shahada (the word of confession of Allah's oneness) these words are rooted in our hearts pronounced by the tongue and practiced by the body there is no compromise for it. If you are in a garden, where prayer has been made in the name of something other than Allah and you say "Amin" then that action negates what you said you believed in and shows the weakness and the level of your Iman (faith). If you are with friends, and *the Adhan* (call to prayer) has been made and you feel reluctant to answer the call of your Creator then your faith is weak. Remember that when you die none of your friends or family will follow you into your grave you will be judged according to your heart's intentions and your deeds alone to answer the reasons why you refused to perform Salah (prayer) when the adhan was called. As a practicing Muslim living in the United States of America, there are two different laws that one has to abide by, (1) The United States Constitutional Laws, both on a Federal level and a Local State level, and (2) The Shari'ah Islamic Laws that are being implemented in Dearborn Michigan of the U.S.

History teaches, us that the founding forefathers of the United States of America gathered in an assembly. To construct a set of convictions known as the ***"Bill of Rights,"*** which consists of the first ten Amendments of the United States Constitution. In doing so, they created a set of convictions namely, the right for its citizens to bear arms, the right to assemble peacefully, and the right to have an attorney appointed when one has been accused of a crime. In an Islamic Country Muslims must abide by a set of laws known as Shari'ah.

When Allah (s.w.t) sent the angel Gabriel (Jibril) to speak to Muhammad (Ahmed, given birth name by his mother) who was not yet a Muslim, the angel Gabriel (Jibril) approached Muhammad (Ahmed, his given name by his mother) and said Iqra (read) at least three times. Still, he proclaimed he did not know how to read. Then Allah made it possible for him to read (Iqra) and understand the language of Arabic by placing the Surah in his heart and this was the very conception of the Shari'ah rule of Law in Al-Islam for the whole of creation to follow the revelations of the Qur'an Muslims and non-Muslims alike. When Muslims are guilty of violating any of the Shari'ah rule of Law they will be judged and convicted according to the crime.

For instance, it's forbidden in Islam to force people to convert and become Muslim, it is prohibited in Islam to deny women and children their rights, and it is not permitted in Islam to enact legal punishments (hudud) without following the correct procedures that ensure justice and Mercy. For Muslims, Shari'ah Law encompasses our values, principles, behaviors, practices, and convictions to uphold the worshipping of Allah (s.w.t), Prayer, Charity, Fasting, and Pilgrimage these laws have all been recorded within the Qur'an but first given to the Prophet Muhammad (*Ahmed, his given name by his mother*) by the permission of Allah through the angel Gabriel.

In the Qur'an, Allah says: (Surah Al-Anbiyaa: 21 [107]

[107] "And we did not send you (O' Muhammad) except as a mercy for all the world."

s a Muslim by choice once, Asiah decided to embrace the Deen (way of life or faith) in Islam she embarked on a conviction of her Ibadah (worship). In doing so, it was Asiah's strong commitment that as a new Muslimah (woman) it would be her duty to adhere to the performance of Salah (prayer) five times per day as instructed by Allah. Asiah would commit herself to helping those less fortunate than herself by performing Zakah (charity) Aiming to ensure that she and other Muslims help each year those in need of assistance. We continue to encourage each other to fast for Ramadan, we must understand that unforeseen circumstances can happen in our daily lives, and it can become difficult for any practicing Muslim to keep up the **_Five Pillars of Islam._** This is one of the reasons why we should surround ourselves with strong-minded practicing Muslims who have a stronger conviction in the Islamic Deen or faith to help keep you on the path to righteousness towards Allah (s.w.t). It has been reported in: Sahih al-Bukhari 5027 Book 66, Virtues of the Qur'an:

Hadith 49 narrated by 'Uthman:

The Prophet (s.a.w.s) said, "The best among you (Muslims) are those who learn the Qur'an and teach it."(Hadith 49)

Allah (s.w.t) has said in the Qur'an to all those who believe.

"O believers! Be the helpers of Allah, just as Isa (Jesus) the son of Maryam said to his disciples: "Who will be my helpers in the cause of Allah?" And the disciples responded: "We will be your helpers in the cause of Allah." Then a group from the children of Israel believed in him (Isa) and another group disbelieved. We aided the believers against their enemies, so they became victorious. (14) (Surah As-Saff 61: [14])

practice the ayah above Allah, (s.w.t) has aided the believer against their enemies therefore if you are among those who have a firmly held belief or conviction about the practice of your Deen (way of Life or faith). As you take the necessary steps towards Allah (s.w.t.) He will aid you in your Ibadah (worship). You shall become successful in practicing **_The Five Pillars of Islam_** and committing to your heart the **_The Articles of Faith._** The entire Muslim Ummah (Community) must adhere to these *Five Pillars of Islam* and the *The Articles of Faith,* no matter what sect they claim to belong. Remember that there is only one Islam, and we shall be called Muslim (One of Peace). Muslims must be steadfast in practicing the performance of Salah (prayer) and Zakah (Charity) for Allah to be pleased with us. As Muslims, we give Sadaqah (Zakah charity) to help the poor, the Orphans, and the needy.

As it so states in the Qur'an. (Surah At-Tauba: 9:[60])

---

(60) "Zakah expenditures are only for the poor and for the needy and for those employed to collect [zakah] and for bringing hearts together [for Islam] and for freeing captives [or slaves] and for those in debt and for the cause of Allah and for the [stranded] traveler-an obligation [imposed] by Allah. And Allah is Knowing and Wise."

May Allah guide those of us who have been blessed with wealth to feel in their hearts a sense of charity to those who are less fortunate than we are Amin!

Wealth is a temporary enjoyment that Allah allows an individual or a group of individual persons to receive, which you cannot take with you in the afterlife of Janna. So, take the time to share your blessings with the less fortunate, the needy, and the poor. So that on the day, the time, and the hour or minutes that Allah calls you to your death and the question is asked of you. What have you done to help those who were less fortunate than you were here on earth, even though nothing is hidden from Allah (s.w.t) at least you will know that your time on earth was not spent in vain and filled with selfishness. Allah will be pleased with you, your heart's intentions, your good deeds and physical actions, and that you were not stingy in the way of your wealth and knowledge. This does not mean that one should deplete their wealth in the task of helping others because you surely need to take care of yourself and your family. Practicing Islam is not at all difficult; it is the behaviors and stereotypes of others that make it difficult but a believer with a strong Islamic conviction can walk through the fire and come out armed with the true knowledge of their Deen or Faith of Islam.

CHAPTER THREE

WHISPERINGS FROM SHAYTAN

(Qur'an Surah Muhammad: 47 Aayah: 1-2)

(1) "Those who disbelieve and obstruct Allah's Way, He will render their deeds fruitless." (2) As for those who believe, and do good deeds, and believe in what is revealed to Muhammad and that is the truth from their Rabb, He will remove from them their sins and improve their condition."

Shaytan, (c.h.) is an open enemy to men and will not stop making efforts to convince you to go back into the darkness after coming into the light of Islam.

As it states in the Qur'an: Surah Al-Baqarah: 2[168-169])

(168) "O mankind, eat from whatever is on earth [that is] lawful and good and do not follow the footsteps of Satan. Indeed, he is to you a clear enemy." (169) "He enjoins you to commit evil and indecency, and to say certain things against Allah about which you do not know."

As a 'New Muslim', you need to understand that the devil has henchmen (followers) among Jinn and men.

(Qur'an Surah; An-Nas: 114[1-6]).

[1] "Say: I seek refuge in the Rabb of mankind,[2] the King of mankind." "[3]the real God of mankind, [4] from the evil of the retreating whisperer (Shaytan or his worker) [5] who whispers into the hearts of mankind,[6] whether he be from among the jinn's or from among mankind."

Sometimes he sends people to you to misguide you, but we must also understand that Allah permits Shaytan to influence us in any way he can, but he is not to take away our free 'will' of choice. These whispers of Shaytan (c.h.) start by painting Islam as a black Faith, by bringing examples of atrocities that had been committed by some Muslims, which is not what Islam commands of them. Some people have accepted Islam not because they are sincere of heart about the faith but because Shaytan whispered in their ears about the acceptance of Islam just so that they could paint it black. There is a Surah in the Quran that speaks of such people Allah refers to them as Kuffar; (Unbelievers) or Munafiqun; (Hypocrites concealers of the truth).

(Qur'an; Al-Ma'idah: 5: [61])

[61] "When they come to you, they say; 'We believe." But unbelievers they come, and unbelievers they departed. Allah knows fully well, what they hide in their hearts."

Shaytan (c.h.) will forever be a whisper to Mankind until Allah (s.w.t) raises him to answer for his crimes. As he informed Allah of such in the *Qur'an, Surah An-Nisa (4:118)* Shaytan has said to Allah that he will take a good portion of Allah's servants and mislead them, he will create false desires within them, and that he will make promises to the servants of Allah to create false desires within. Remember that Shaytan's promises are tactics he used to deceive you and to keep you from your path of righteousness. Too, stop you from continuing your righteous walk towards Allah. When you start to hear whispers of going astray, read the story in the Qur'an or the Bible about how Satan (may Allah curse him) tempted Adam and Eve.

(Qur'an, Al-Baqarah: 2[35-36] It says,

> (35) "To Adam we said: Dwell with your wife in Paradise and eat anything you want from its bountiful food from wherever you wish, but do not approach this tree, or you shall both become transgressors."
>
> (36) "But Shaytan tempted them with the tree to disobey Allah's commandment and caused them to slip therefrom (paradise) and get them expelled from where they were. We said: "Get down from here, some of you being enemies to others, and there is for you in the earth an abode and provisions for a specified period."

For instance, Shaytan the rebellious one, will have people believe that all Muslims are terrorists. The Acts of terrorism and the killing of innocent souls by proclaiming they are committing such acts all in the name of Allah and Islam. This is the work of Shaytan and his promises to mislead and make use of deceptive tactics to cause you to go astray, in an attempt to put some of his followers, in the forefront of Islam for him to become successful in the destruction of Islam. These types of actions can distract you from your Islamic Deen and may cause you to walk away from being a practicing Muslim. One should establish an understanding of what Islam represents, and what is required of you as a Muslim. This will help you to understand why some of us who have taken their shahada, became Muslims but are not practicing their faith according to Allah's commandments, and the Sunnah of Islam. They may do things not instructed by Allah (s.w.t.) and His Prophet Muhammad (Ahmed given name by his mother), of Islam. Now with an established clear understanding and the knowledge you are gaining about Islam, this can help you to refute anyone who attempts to bring issues to you about the negative actions some Muslims display in Islam. With the truth, you could lead them to the light of righteousness by dismantling their preconception of Islam and being a model Muslim.

Not all Muslims adhere to the principles of Islam, such as the 'Five Pillars' and 'The Articles of Faith.' You can strengthen your faith by reading the Qur'an in your language and learning to read it in Arabic.

Your first line of defense as being a 'New Muslim' is to read the Qur'an with the understanding of its revelations for following Islamic practices, then there are the Hadiths written by Scholars such as Sahih Bukhari and Muslim and the Scholar Imam Abu Zakaria Mohiuddin author of (Riyad-us-Saliheen) a compilation of Hadith Books with reference from the Qur'an. Remember to ensure that any Hadiths you read, are referencing what the Holy Qur'an is saying in comparison.

These are the true references we need to turn our attention to, and not turn our attention to just anyone who professes to be Muslim. Because when they are speaking to you about Islam and they are not making mention of the Qur'an, or of what has been reported of the Prophet Muhammad, s.a.w.s. (Ahmed, his given name by his mother) and show you where the information can best be found. Then what is the use of them relaying such information to you about how to be a Muslim and how to practice Islam successfully?

(Qur'an Surah Baqarah: 2:137)

So, ⁽¹³⁷⁾ "if they believe (accept Islam) like you have believed they shall be rightly guided; if they reject it, they will surely fall into dissension (divide into differing factions); Allah will be your sufficient defender against them, and He hears and knows everything."

Therefore, we must have the correct intentions when we accept Islam and all that is required of us as striving practicing Muslims. If one holds onto the rope of Allah, (s.w.t.) then in our sincere worship, He, Allah will guide us in our Deen-ul Islam. Remember that our Iman (faith) is with the intentions of our hearts and not so much our words of intentions because Allah (s.w.t.) looks at our heart's intention on the Day of Judgment and we will therefore be judged according to our heart's intention and our deeds. Allah (s.w.t) does not give reverence to the looks of a Muslim but this does not mean we should not dress according to the Quranic instruction of how we should dress and behave in this life. Our dress is our identity for others to know that we are Muslim. It sets us apart from anyone else in this world. It allows others to know that we are Muslims even when we fall short of practicing all of the 'Five Pillars of Islam.' Others will never know but your appearance will surely alert them if you are Muslim or not. So don't allow Shaytan (c.h.) to whisper in your ears making *'Haram'* things and behaviors appear great while also making *'Halal'* things and behaviors appear bad or unacceptable. Our identity as Muslims is shown in our character, behavior, and mannerisms towards those who are not Muslims, giving them a model to live by.

[Al-Hujuraat: 49: 13] says.

> "O mankind! We have created you from a male and a female, and made you into nations and tribes, so that you may know one another. Verily, the most honorable of you with Allah is that (believer) who has At-Taqwa [i.e., he is one of the Muttaquun (the pious)]. Verily, Allah is All-Knowing, All-Aware."

Remember that some intentions may appear good, but the person may mean it for your bad. So, you must beware of those who clothe themselves in sheep's clothing to gain your favor or friendship. It has been narrated in. Al-Sahih that Abu Hurayrah said: "The Messenger of Allah (s.a.w.s) said; "Allah does not look at your appearance or your wealth, but He looks at your hearts and your deeds." (Narrated by Muslim, Al-Birr wa'l-Silah, 651)

Quran Surah Al-Ahzab: 33: [59].

> (59) "O Prophet! Enjoin your wives, daughters, and the believing women that they should draw their gowns over themselves. That is more proper, so that they may be recognized and not bothered. Allah is Forgiving, Merciful."

As Muslim women and non-Muslim women in general we should dress so that we are recognized as Muslim or honorable women, and not dress so that others would view or treat us as prostitutes for their sinful means and disrespect us for dressing as loose women. Iblis (Shaytan, c.h.) does a wonderful job of keeping his promise to Allah (s.w.t) about making terrible things seem good and good things seem bad. Remember that Shaitan has no power over human beings, he only invites people to follow because Mankind was created weak.

In the Qur'an Surah Ibrahim/Abraham: 14 [22] Shaitan admits to having no power over human beings and he admits that he just invited mankind to commit the wrong and that it is mankind who accepts his invitations.

Qur'an Surah Ibrahim: 14 [22]

(22) "And the devil will say when the matter is decided: Surely Allah promised you a promise of truth, and I promised you and then failed you. And I had no authority over you, except that I called you and you obeyed me; so, blame me not but blame yourselves. Cannot come for your help, nor can you come to my help. Denied your associating me with Allah before. Surely for the unjust is a painful chastisement."

Now this is nothing but the truth being confirmed by the whispering of Shaitan (the cursed one) who admits to leading Mankind with deception. So, you shall learn, and understand Allah is not the deceiver of humanity nor is Allah leading you astray.(Ih'dna al-sirata al-mus'taqima), guide us to the straightway, Allah will guide you to the straight path, but he will allow you to go astray if you so wish and no one can bring you back to the right path accept Allah, through your worship of Him, your repentance for going astray, and asking that he lead you back on the path of righteousness, while keeping Shaitan from whispering in your ear. Shaytan is keeping the promise made to Allah (s.w.t) that he would cause humanity and the jinn to sin by "Insinuating whisper"(waswasa) in their hearts (qalb)

Meaning whispers that are coming from Shaytan, and the (waswasah) coming from the (Nafs) soul. Surah Nas 114/1-6 of the Quran Ayahs 4 says.

Shaytan's Whisper to Mankind and Jinn

Say. "I seek refuge with (Allah) the Lord of mankind, 'The King of mankind, 'The Ilah (God) of mankind, (4) 'From the evil of the whisperer (devil who whispers evil in the hearts of men) who withdraws (from his whispering in one's heart after one remembers Allah), "Who whispers in the breasts of mankind, "Of jinn's and men."

Due to the transient nature of life in the Dunyah (Earth), as opposed to the eternal realm of the afterlife, known as "akhirah," when you start to hear whispers in your heart trying to sway you away from the guidance of Allah (s.w.t.) Recite Surah 114 Nas, which Allah revealed to the Prophet (s.a.w.s) to safeguard him from the whispers of Shaytan while he was under a magical enchantment, according to a hadith.

CHAPTER FOUR

MISCONCEPTION ABOUT ISLAM

Some of the terms used in Islam that new Muslims should acquire and understand are as follows:

Fard:	Compulsory or Obligatory
Halal:	Allow or Permissible
Haraam:	Prohibited or Forbidden
Makruh:	Not Recommended or Discourage
Mubah:	Permissible or Allowed
Mustahab:	Recommended or Encourage

AS, Asiah was beginning to practice, Deen-ul Islam, or Faith of Islam, as a New Muslim there were so many opinions about the wearing of the Hijab for Muslim women and the covering of her face. The misconception for non-Muslims and Muslims alike is that in Islam women are compelled to dawn the face veil. Well, there is no compulsion in the Islamic faith in terms of wearing the face veil, it's by choice not by force

Quran Surah (Baqarah: 2: 256).

⁽²⁵⁶⁾ "Let there be no compulsion in faith."

In Asiah's studies, she have learned that the sole purpose of wearing the hijab is so that women will not become sexual targets of men. Allah (s.w.t), decided to instruct women to cover the parts of their body that would be so appealing to men. This would stop them from being harassed when walking down the streets, even though some Muslim women are still harassed by men who don't care. Because such a man feels women are beneath them. Allah (s.w.t) also created this law instructing the women to cover their bosoms because the wives of Prophet Muhammad, (Ahmed, his given name by his mother) (salla Allaahu 'alayhi wa salaam) needed to be distinguished among the other women. They needed to be seen and known as the best of women kind so for this reason, Allah, (s.w.t) commanded the Prophet Muhammad (s.a.w.s).

(Qur'an Al—Ahzab: 33: 59)

Prophet! Enjoin your wives, daughters, and the believing women that they should draw their gowns over themselves. That is more proper, so that they may be recognized and not bothered. Allah is Forgiving, Merciful." ⁽⁵⁹⁾

For instance, Aisha (a.s.), one of the Prophets' wives had false accusations levied against her while traveling in the desert. If you read Surah 24, ayah 11 through 13 in the Qur'an you will find the story about Aisha (a.s.) the youngest wife of the Prophets (s.a.w.s.).

Qurán Sura 24: 11-13 states:

(11) "Surely, those who concocted the slander (against 'Aisha—a wife of the Prophet) are from a clique among you. Do not regard this incident as only evil, for it also contains a good lesson for you. Whoever took any part in this sin has earned their share accordingly, and the one who took on himself the leading part shall have a terrible punishment." (12) "Why did not the believing men and believing women, when they heard of this slander, think well of their people, and say: "This is clearly a false accusation?" (13)"Why did they not produce four witnesses? If they cannot produce the required witnesses, they are the liars in the sight of Allah."

So, as you can see from the ayahs above, the slandering of any person is not in the best interest of mankind, especially if you have no valid proof. Allah (s.w.t) clearly understood this to be the best way to keep all believing Muslim women from harassment by men on the street or in the workplace because they are dressed in modesty. In *Surah An-Nur: 24:30* Allah revealed some measures of prevention for the men to also dress with modesty and *24:31* for the women about hijab. Allah (s.w.t) measures of prevention by giving the Prophet Muhammad, s.a.w.s. (Ahmed, his given name by his mother) these instructions both for men and women when He said.

Men

(30)"Tell the believing men to lower their gaze and guard their modesty; that is purer for them. Surely, Allah is well aware of their actions."

Women

(31)"And for the believing women to "lower their gaze and guard their modesty; not to display their beauty and ornaments except what normally appears thereof (Face and Hands); let them draw their veils over their bosoms and not display their adornment..."

Then there is the misconception about polygamy in Islam the misunderstanding that a Muslim man must take more than one wife. Having more than one wife in Islam is neither compulsory nor obligatory. In truth Allah, (s.w.t) in the Qur'an is giving the Muslim men a strong recommendation and encouragement on marriage of women and how to treat them especially orphan and slave girls they wish to marry.

Qur'an (Surah An-Nisa 4[3])

(3)"If you fear that you shall not be able to treat the orphans with fairness, then marry other women of your choice; two, three, or four. But if you fear that you will not be able to maintain justice between your wives, then marry only one or any slave girl you may own. That will be more suitable, so that you may not deviate from the Right Way."

Accepting polygamy in Islam for some women is not an easy fate because it is difficult to control their emotions let alone understand why their husband wishes to marry another wife. Muslim men do not make it easy as well because they like to play games of deception. Some men do not expose the fact they do have a first wife. Example: Asiah's ex-husband Usman has a first wife and when they met, he did tell her about his first wife, he introduced them, but she was not interested in meeting Asiah or knowing anything about her. Usman's first wife was not pleasant for someone who is supposed to be a practicing Muslim woman Asiah summed her reaction up to her not wanting him to have a second wife. Then there is the other side of this equation the Muslim man who goes ahead and marries a second wife without informing his first wife about that second wife until he is already married, this type of behavior will cause tension between the two wives.

Polygamy is a great asset to the Ummah (Community) for the family. It is a great resource in helping out the other co-wife with her children, and the chores of the house provided you and your co-wife live in the same abode. The persistent pressure from the husband to fulfill his intimacy needs can create a challenging situation for the wife. In cases where one wife is not interested in being intimate with her husband, it is resolved by the fact that he has another wife. "If both husband and wife are faithful, it can reduce the risk of diseases. However, if a man is not financially able to support a second wife, he should follow the guidance of Allah (s.w.t) and remain with one wife.

Even when you read the other scriptural books, the Torah and the Injeel you will notice nowhere in these Holy Books does it instruct man to take only one wife. Ibrahim (Abraham) had three wives (Sarah, Hagar, and Keturah) according to *Genesis 25:1* Ibrahim took another wife after the death of his first wife Sarah, and King Solomon had many wives, but the Qur'anic Surah An-Nisa: 4: [3] advise that man take only one wife if equality is unattainable. The misconception that Allah, (s.w.t), or the Prophet (s.a.w.s), instructed that a Muslim man must have more than one wife is not true, this is a choice given to men and not to be taught as compulsory in Islam. Therefore, under Islam, a woman cannot demand that her husband not have a second wife or be forced to accept that he has a second wife; she must either accept polygamy in her life or ask for a divorce if she does not want to agree. However, the best recourse is for the wife to relay her concerns of not wanting her husband to take a second wife within their marriage contract.

In no way is Asiah saying that any Muslim woman should seek separation from her husband through divorce. However, if you as a Muslim woman are not willing to understand or accept that your husband desires to take another wife then divorce is the right of any Muslim woman.

The Prophet Muhammad, s.a.w.s. (Ahmed, his given name by his mother) was the only human being permitted to marry more than four wives because of warring times when a wife became a widow with children to care for and the husband was killed fighting for the cause of Islam, Prophet Muhammad, (s.a.w.s) was allowed to marry them, and he could not divorce any of them because he wanted to marry another.

It is stated in the Quran. (Surah Al-Ahzab: 33 [50])

(50)"O Prophet, We have made lawful your wives whom you have given their dowries, and those whom your right hand possesses, out of those whom Allah has given you as prisoners of war…"

Then again in Qur'an Allah decreed these words to the Prophet Muhammad s.a.w.s (Ahmed, given birth name by his mother).

(Surah Al-Ahzab: 33:[52])

(52)"It is not allowed for you to take wives after this, nor to change them for other wives, though their beauty is pleasing to you, except those whom your right hand possesses. And Allah is ever Watchful over all things."

Once when the wives (a.s.) of The Prophet (s.a.w.s) caused him to become angry he gave them two options they were (1) to be divorced or (2) to stay with him, this took place after one month of being away from his wives then Allah (s.w.t) revealed these

Ayah's in Surah Al-Ahzab: 33 [ayahs; 28-29], to Prophet Muhammad s.a.w.s (Ahmed, his given birth name by his mother) for his wives to choose.

Qurán Al-Ahzab 33 : 28-29

> (28)"If they desire this world's life and its adornment, come, I will give you a provision and allow you to depart a goodly departing."
>
> (29) "And if they desire Allah and His Messenger and the abode of the Hereafter, then surely Allah has prepared for the doers of good among you mighty reward."

They turned down the option of divorcing the Messenger for worldly gains; instead, they all chose Allah, marriage to the Prophet, and an abode (home) in the afterlife (Paradise) on the last days on earth.

Now instead of viewing polygamy as an intrusion into your life of marriage perhaps you can view it as a resource of help in your life, most times accepting a co-wife can be the very blessing you were looking for as a sister, a friend, someone you can trust as a believer in the 'Five Pillars of Islam' and the 'Articles of Faith.' The instruction within the Qur'an does not encourage polygamy it seems more on the side of discouraging the behavior as a measure of preventing the believer from swaying to the left of an unjust behavior amongst his wives and for so many of these good reasons (fairness, equality, economically and emotionally). Besides, there are many other reasons a man may want to marry a second wife, and here are a few.

- ❖ His first wife after several years may not have borne him any children.
- ❖ He and his first wife may have children, but she has taken ill, or perhaps Allah, (s.w.t.) has called her home.
- ❖ His first wife agrees with having a co-wife.

❖ He may be away on assignment to a new job and the first wife did not wish to join him in another country, so he married another wife to keep from committing Zina (adultery, or fornication).

Treating your wives justly is the principal factor and being financially able to support more than one is your decision.

Qur'an Surah: 4:129, pg.205)

(129)"It is not for you to do perfect justice between your wives even if you wish to do so; therefore, to comply with Divine Laws, do not lean towards one wife to the extent that you leave the other hanging in the air (neither married nor divorced). If you work out a friendly understanding and fear Allah, Allah is forgiving Merciful."

There is a Hadith Volume 7, Book 62 Number 27 by Sahih Al-Bukhari (2009).

Narrated by Abu Huraira, reporting the Prophet as saying,

"A woman is married for four things (i.e., her wealth, her family status, her beauty, and her faith), so you should marry the religious woman (otherwise) you will be a loser." **(pg. 1138)**

So, men in Islam don't marry women for reasons of lust or usury because Allah, knows your true intentions, He is The Seer of all things hidden. There are many more reasons than what Asiah has mentioned but rest assured that there are more women on this earth than there are men which is why so much fornication and adultery is being committed. There are several other reasons for the lack of men in the realm of sexual preference of some men and women to be in committed relationships with the same sex preference, which is <u>*Haraam*</u> in Islam and any other faith as well it is prohibited or forbidden in the Torah, and the Injeel this I know for sure. Then there is the incarceration of both men and women. Just know that Allah gave us free will of choice to do what we like in this world, and he will judge you in the hereafter and decide your punishment for the choices you make in this earthly life. Keep in mind that Allah Created Mankind and Jinn to worship him alone.

The Qur'an states in Surah 4: 26-28

(26)"Allah desires to clarify and guide you to the ways which were followed by the righteous people before you and turn to you in mercy. Allah is the knowledgeable, Wise."

(27)"Allah wishes to forgive you, but those who follow their lusts wish to see you deviate far away from the Right Way."

(28)"Allah wishes to lighten your burdens because humans have been created weak by nature."

As you follow, your new path towards an Islamic journey. With evidentiary concluded research, you will start understanding the misconceptions about Islam. As for Asiah, she does not judge the faith or life of anyone. She aims to illuminate her experiences as a new Muslim, managing challenges with prayer instead of anger. Asiah decided to gain knowledge about her Deen (way of life or faith) in Islam. So that she could become a model Muslim and show others where to locate the truth for themselves. Once someone is illuminated, by the light of truth it offers a greater understanding of Asiah's experience when Allah (s.w.t) illuminated her with the light of truth at the age of nine. No one else has the power to lead you astray or bring you back to Islam except Allah (Subhanna wa Ta'ala). Therefore, continue to walk towards Allah (s.w.t) in a virtuous manner, while maintaining your faith and holding on to His guidance. Keep those who spread negativity away from influencing you and distance yourself from their harmful words. Ask Allah for protection from such people when performing Salah (prayer) over all forces that wish to call you towards the temptation of 'Haram' acts.

Recite these words when you feel negative energy attempting to still your peace and harmony. Ask for protection from Shaytain and his numerous followers.

"I seek refuge with Allah, the All-Hearing, and the All-Knowing from Shaitan, the accursed." (A'uoodhu bil-laahis samee'il 'aleemi minash-shaitaanir-rajeem)

CHAPTER FIVE

THE DUTIES OF A MUSLIM

(Qur'an Al-'idah: 5:48)

(48) "...We have ordained a law and a way of life for each of you. If Allah wanted, He could have made all of you a single nation. But He willed otherwise to test you in what He has given you, therefore, try to excel one another in good deeds. You all shall return to Allah; then He will tell you the truth of those matters in which you dispute..."

Becoming a Muslim is not the end of your journey but the beginning of your journey to paradise. The first duty of a 'New Muslim is to understand what Islam is about. Islam is a Deen or faith based on knowledge and evidence from authentic sources. Dogmatism (stubborn and narrow-mindedness) and blind fellowship (prejudice and bigotry) are not part of Islam.

Islam is like that of a tree with many branches or like that of a library, which has a wealth of knowledgeable sources of information, the trick is in knowing how to select the correct information of knowledge you seek.

About your Duty as a Muslim:

It is your duty as a Muslim to learn how to read and understand the Qur'an in its original form Arabic. Whenever you read the Qur'an in a language that you can understand. Obtaining an understanding of the Arabic language can assist you in identifying and understanding the translations which would give new meaning to what you are reciting each time you perform Salah (prayer) or even study the Qur'an at your leisure. As you will begin to identify and match the Arabic words with the corresponding words in the language that you speak. Some Arabic words cannot be transcribed into other languages because there is no word equivalent of which you will learn. Knowing how to read and understand the Hadith, and the acts of worship, fundamentals of Aqeeda (Islamic beliefs), it was reported that the Prophet Muhammad s.a.w.s, (Ahmed, his given birth name by his mother), *said.*

Sahih Muslim

"Whoever seeks a way to acquire knowledge Allah will make easy his way to Paradise." **[(2699)]**

You must seek knowledge for learning because the wealth of knowledge continues until you no longer exist in this earthly realm. Remember if you "acquire knowledge Allah will make Paradise easy." therefore learning about Islam never stops.

A striving Muslim's second duty is of equal importance, It is putting into practice what you have learned. It is not about accumulating knowledge it is about how you practice what you have learned daily. During the initial stages of Islam, there are reports that the Sahaba (Companions) would come to the Prophet (s.a.w.s) to learn only 10 verses from the Qur'an, commit them to memory, and put them into practice after which they would learn another 10 verses. It was reported that one Sahabi (Companion) after reading, Surah 24 ayahs 27-28 of the Qur'an reads as follows:

Suratul An-Nur: 24:[27-28], where Allah said.

---

(27)"O believers! Do not enter houses other than your own until you have sought permission and said greetings of peace to the occupants. This is better for you, so that you may be mindful."

(28)"If you do not find anybody therein, still, do not enter until permissions are given to you; and if you are asked to go back, then go back; this is more fitting for you, and Allah is cognizant of what you do."

These reports state that a certain Sahabi (Companion) stood up and started visiting people asking for permission to come into their homes. They all said yes, except for one. When the Sahabi (Companion), reached the house of this man he requested his permission to enter the man's home as ordered in the Quran Surah An-Nur: 24 ayahs, (27-28) the man denied the request of the Sahabi (Companion) and asked that he go back because he did not wish to receive visitors now.

The reports say that the Sahabi (Companion) was so delighted to have been turned away that in utterance to himself, he said; "yes, I was able to practice this portion of the Qur'an which said go back if you are asked to go back. Good that I have someone that will at least say go back."

These are simple teachings of Islam, but today if we knock at someone's door and they say please I don't need visitors, are we going to become offended when this is an option in the Qur'an? Many practicing Muslims and non-Muslims alike think it's rude and offensive to them when someone wishes not to invite them into their homes. We should not take offense because the Qur'an teaches us how to handle this type of situation as you have read from the above ayah.

On the subject of lending and borrowing money from family and friends, it is your duty as a Muslim to follow what is written within the Qur'an about these matters.

To ensure that the lender and the recipient obtain full justice in terms of the agreed-upon financial amount, leaving no opportunity for discussion or disagreement on the terms of return, Allah commands, in plain language, that all financial agreements be established in writing.

Al-Baqarah: 2:(282)

"O believers! When you deal with each other in lending for a fixed period, of time put it in writing. Let a scribe write it down with justice between the parties."

If someone wants to borrow money, you need to ensure the return of your money by requesting the individual put their signature on a contract of liability (debtor). Ensure also that you have a witness besides Allah (s.w.t) they may become offended thinking that you lost trust in them. This particular action is a Muslim's duty according to what the Quranic verse clearly instructs you as the lender and the other person as the borrower. It is a simple instruction from Allah (s.w.t). It is a means of bringing peace and tranquility. Sometimes we become discouraged by the behavior of other Muslims who so often feel the need to challenge the way we practice our Islamic Deen or faith. All that you need to do to ensure that you are on the correct path of righteousness is to provide proof for anything you wish to do, and this will build up your confidence as a striving 'New Muslim.' Be a model for Islam because now that you are a Muslim all eyes will be on you. Watching your every step closely and people will always have something to say or offer you some sort of advice. Be pleasant about it, listen to the advice, and then research what you were told. When you find any discrepancies bring it to the attention of the individual Muslim who gave you the information. Approach them with the same character as that of the Prophet (s.a.w.s) would have and be humble in correcting them. Solve, resolve and sort matters out amicably, and whenever there are issues handle them most respectfully to follow the character of the Prophet (s.a.w.s) besides it is your duty as a Muslim to promote and practice peace in Islam.

Then there is the duty placed upon every Muslim to spread the good news about Islam in a way that would encourage others to develop a curiosity about the peaceful way you are practicing your religious Deen Islam. How you carry yourself around others as a Muslim, you also must wear appropriate clothing, covering all that is enticing to the male or female. For women wearing the hijab is for the protection of your modesty, your hijab should also cover your bosom (breast) and for men according to the Qur'an (Kufi head cap) is for them to wear loose-fitting clothing that will not display the private parts of their body.

Guidance for Dressing Properly An-Nur: 24 ayahs, 30-31)

Men

[30] "Enjoin the believing men to lower their gaze and guard their modesty; that is a chaser for them. Surely, Allah is well aware of their actions."

Women

[31] "Likewise, enjoin the believing women to lower their gaze and guard their modesty; not to display their beauty and ornaments except what normally appears thereof; let them draw their veils over their booms and not display their adornments except to their husbands..."

Now many Muslim women wear the face veil most because this is what their husbands have requested and others because they chose to do so. However, Allah; has not made the wearing of the face veil (Obligatory) in Islam the wearing of the face veil is

(Voluntary). So rather, you wear the face veil for yourself or at the request of your husband, it is by choice and not by force.

It says in the Qur'an. (Suratul Al-Baqarah: 2: (256)

> (256) "There is no compulsion in faith; true guidance has been made clearly distinct from error. Therefore, whoever renounces 'Taghoot' (false deities – Shaytan) and believes in Allah has grasped the firm handhold that will never break. Allah, whose handhold you have grasped, hears all and knows all,"

So, remember this verse in the Qur'an when someone tells you that you must wear the face veil which Islam does not make compulsory or obligatory as a condition for being a practicing Muslim. Then there is your duty as a 'New Muslim to learn and memorize the Surahs of the Qur'an in Arabic and the meaning in your language to obtain a clear understanding of what you are saying and obtain the ability to perform Salah (prayer) in the original language of Arabic with a clear understanding of what you are reciting. Here are some recommendations of Surah's to begin your memorization of the Qur'an.

They are as follows; Suratul Fatihah is the beginning of the Holy Qur'an but before you recite Suratul Fatihah the 'Basmala' which is (Bismil-laahir Rahmaanir Raheem), is recited at the beginning of every Surah accept one Surah At-Tawba: (9) this is the only Surah without the opening words of the 'Basmala' (Bismil-laahir Rahmaanir Raheem), is not recited at the beginning of this particular Surah because it is said that the Prophet (s.a.w.s) had not dictated it.

Surah Al-Fatihah: 1 "Supplication to Allah for guidance taught by Allah Himself."

("Bismil-laahir Rahmaanir Raheem")

1. Alhamdul lillahi rabbil 'alAAalameen
2. Alrrahmani alrraheemi

3. Maliki yawmi alddeeni
4. Iyyaaka na'budu wa iyyaaka nasta'een
5. Ihdinas siratal mstaqeem
6. Siraatal ladheena an 'amta Alai-him,
7. Ghayri maghduubi Alayhim walad aldalleena.

("In the name of Allah, the Yielder, the Merciful").

All praise is for Allah, the Rabb of the Worlds. (2)The Yielder, the Merciful, (3) Master of the Day of Judgment, (4) You alone we worship, and you alone we call on for help, (5) Guide us to The Right path, (6) The path of those whom thou hast favored, (7)not the (path) of those who earn thine anger nor of those who go astray." ***(Qur'an 1: [1-7])***

❖ Surah Al-'ASR: 103 "Formula for the way to salvation."

("Bismil-laahir Rahmaanir Raheem")

1. WaalAasr
2. Inna al-insana lafee khusr
3. Illa allatheena amanoo waAamiloo alssalihati watawasaw bialhaqqi watawasaw bissabr.

("In the name of Allah, the Yielder, the Merciful").

"By the time, (2) Indeed, mankind is in loss, (3)Except those who have believed and done righteous deeds and advised each other to truth and advised each other to patience.") **(Qur'an 103: [1-3])**

❖ *Surah Al-Kafirun: 109* "The commandment not to compromise in the matters of faith."

("Bismil-laahir Rahmaanir Raheem")

1. ul ya ayyuha alkafirun
2. La aAAbudu ma taAAbuduun
3. Wala antum AAabiduuna maaAAbud
4. Wala ana AAabidun maAAbadtum
5. Wala antum AAabiduuna maaAAbud
6. Lakum deenukum waliya deen.

("In the name of Allah, the Yielder, the Merciful")

Say; O unbelievers, (2) I do not worship that, which you worship, (3) nor do you worship that which I worship, (4) I shall never worship that which you worship, (5) nor will you ever worship that which I worship. (6) You have your faith, and I have mine." **(Qur'an 109: [1-6])**

❖ *Surah An-Nasr: 110* "Victory comes with the help of Allah."

("Bismil-laahir Rahmaanir Raheem")

1. Itha jaa nasru Allahiwalfath
2. Waraayta annasa yadkhuloonafee deeni Allahi afwaja
3. Fasabbih bihamdi rabbika wastaghfirhuinnahu kana tawwaba.

("In the name of Allah, the Yielder, the Merciful")

"When Allah helps and the victory comes, (2) and you see people embracing Allah's faith (Islam) in multitudes. (3) So, glorify forgiveness: surely, He is ever ready to accept the repentance and forgive. (Qur'an 110: [1-3])

❖ *Surah Al-Ikhlas: 112* "Tawheed – the unique attribute of Allah."

    ("Bismil-laahir Rahmaanir Raheem")
1. Qul huwa Allahu ahad
2. Allahu ssamad
3. Lam yalid walam yulad
4. Walam yakun lahu kufuwan ahad.

    ("In the name of Allah, the Yielder, the Merciful").

(1)Say: "He Allah is one. (2) Allah is self-sufficient, (3) He begets not, nor is He begotten, (3) and there is none comparable to Him." **(Qur'an 112: [1-4])**

❖ *Surah Al-Falaq: 113* "Seek refuge with Allah from the slinking whisperers."

    ("Bismil-laahir Rahmaanir Raheem")
1. Qul Aauuthu birabbi alfalaq
2. Min sharri ma khalaqa
3. Wamin sharri ghasiqin itha waqaba
4. Wamin sharri annaffathatifee alAuqad
5. Wamin sharri hasidin itha hasad.

    ("In the name of Allah, the Yielder, the Merciful").

(1)Say, "I seek refuge in the Lord of daybreak, (2)From the evil of that which He has created, (3) And from the evil of darkness when it settles. (4) And from the evil of those who blow in knots. (5) And from the evil of an envier when he envies."

(Qur'an 113: [1-5])

❖ *Surah An-Nas: 114* "Seek refuge with Allah from the slinking whisperers."

("Bismil-laahir Rahmaanir Raheem")

1. Qul aAuthu birabbi alnnasa
2. Maliki alnnasa
3. Ilahi alnnasa
4. Min sharri al-was-was al-khannasi.
5. Al-lathee yu-waswisu fee suduuri alnnasa
6. Mina-al jinnati wa alnnasm.

("In the name of Allah, the Yielder, the Merciful").

⁽¹⁾Say, "I seek refuge in the Rabb of mankind. ⁽²⁾The Sovereign of mankind, ⁽³⁾The God of mankind, ⁽⁴⁾From the evil of the retreating whisperer, ⁽⁵⁾Who whispers [evil] into the breasts of mankind, ⁽⁶⁾From among the jinn and mankind." **(Quran 114: [1-6])**

These particular Surahs are but a few of which you should work on memorizing. It will not be an easy task but if you study and practice every day you will become successful at reciting Qur'anic Surahs correctly.

Many online websites can help you to read, write, and recite the Surah's of the Qur'an like ***www.SearchTruth.com*** this website has a wealth of Islamic information that you would be comfortable with, and the download is free, and you can also submit a donation of what you can afford. So just, relax in knowing that all will be well as you go through your journey and your walk towards Allah (s.w.t), the Sunnah, and the Qur'an, which is the last conformational revelation, given to the Prophet Muhammad, s.a.w.s. (Ahmed, his given name by his mother), from Allah through the Angel Gabriel, (pbuh).

"No matter how long you have been practicing the Deen (way of life or faith) of Islam, all Muslims should consider themselves as "New Muslims" because every day Allah bestows his continued blessing of life upon us as He allows us to awaken from our rest. We are given another opportunity to renew our Iman (faith) and our Ibadah (worship) to Him alone" This should be done until we have reached our final stages in this life on our way to Jannah (Hereafter, Paradise), Insha Allah (If Allah wills)."Here are a few special Scholars who dedicated their lives to the Fiqh of (Islamic Jurisprudence) Islam; they are known as the four Imams' (Leaders) who started their studies at a very young age in life. "It doesn't mean you can't study and learn Islamic Jurisprudence. You need to understand that it takes a lifetime to learn. That's why the Prophet (s.a.w.s) said that whoever seeks knowledge will earn a place in Paradise. All Muslims should seek knowledge from the cradle to the grave."

The Four Famous Imams of Fiqh:
- Imam Abu Hanifa and the name of his school of Fiqh (School of Law)
- Imam Malik- The Scholar of Madinah his school of Fiqh (Maliki Madhab school)
- Imam Al-Shafi'I – The Father of Usul Al-Fiqh and the name of his school of Fiqh (Usul Al-Fiqh school)
- Imam Ahmad Ibn Hanbal—The Champion of Islamic Belief his school of Fiqh (school of thought).

"The scholars of Fiqh are some of the best in their field, and every Muslim needs to read about these four scholars and compare their teachings.

They learned from each other and improved the studies and teachings of one another. Usman and Asiah also recommend you read the Hadiths of Imams Sahih Al-Bukhari and Sahih Muslim to learn about 'The Science of Hadith.'

CHAPTER SIX

SUBMITTING ONESELF TO ALLAH

(Qur'an Ali-'Imran: 3:84)

(84) "O Prophet, say: We believe in Allah and what is revealed to us and what was revealed to Ibrahim (Abraham), Isma'il (Ishmael), Ishaq (Isaac), Ya'qoob (Jacob) and the Descendants (the Prophets who were the offspring of Jacob): and in that which was given to Musa (Moses), Isa (Jesus) and other Prophets from their Rabb; we do not discriminate between any one of them, and to Allah do we submit ourselves as Muslims."

Islam means total submission to the will of Allah, as a "New Muslim", you need to understand that only in submitting oneself to our Creator Allah (s.w.t), will humanity obtain spiritual peace. When we are requested to submit ourselves to Allah it simply means for all those who profess their oneness, (*Laa ilaaha illa Allah)*, there is no Creator besides Allah, we should allow Allah to take total control of our lives and our destiny.

The Qur'an has been sent as a Guidance to prevent mankind from walking through the murky waters of life however, because Allah allowed us to have free will unlike the angels who have no choice but to submit and do as Allah requests of them. Allah has given us as human beings the opportunity to make choices of our free will, so long as we are living here in the Dunyah (world), until such time 'He calls us to our death on the Day of Judgment to answer for our deeds both good and bad. But Allah truly created mankind and Jinn to submit to him and nothing else, human beings were created as weak vessels.

There is no decision you will make in this lifetime, without asking yourself if this is what Allah has commanded us to do through His scriptures, Prophets, Messengers, and the Sunnah of Islam. Islam is a faith of comprehension that speaks about every aspect of our lives. Islam covers every decision that one can make whether it is 'haram' or 'halal' Allah sent Qur'anic surahs and Ayahs that give us detailed instructions on how to prevent making bad decisions, and how to achieve true peace and distribute justice among mankind. The Qur'an also helps striving Muslims, and those who are non-Muslims resolve issues in our worldly affairs and advises us on whom we should associate ourselves with.

The instructions within the Qur'an are unquestionable without doubt straightforward to the point. Allah (s.w.t) is not about deception that is the life of Iblis (Shaytan, c.h.) the greatest whispers of deception to take you off the beaten path of your righteous walk towards Allah.

Even if we don't understand the motivations behind the enactment of these laws like putting limitations on the number of wives one man could marry the subtle advice on being intoxicated while performing Salah (prayer) or why one action is no longer permissible and what once was permissible is now prohibited, just remember that Allah knows better than we do. Take a step back and do some research on the pre-

Islamic errors and learn about their behaviors and the endless number of wives and maidens who were being mistreated during those pre-Islamic years.

The earlier Muslims accepted the rulings of Islam without question because they had the opportunity to witness the atrocities of burying infant females alive the total disregard for the thoughts of any woman and the lying and cheating as well as the worshipping of many 'gods' or Deities. The pre-Islamic error just disregarded all that Allah (s.w.t) had sent through the previous Prophets and Messengers before the last Prophet Muhammad, s.a.w.s (Ahmed, his given name by his mother).

In these, modern times there is scientific evidence that has shed more light on the benefits of practicing Islam. For example, when people attempt to justify their reasons for eating certain foods that are prohibited and the ingestion of alcohol when it, is prohibited by Allah (s.w.t). In the Qur'an Surah Baqarah, has a list of categories that are in line with the Divine Laws that explain what is **permissible or prohibited, and obligatory or recommended** in Islam. The excitement felt when reading Surah Baqarah stems from the fact that each time it is read, a piece of deeper knowledge is gained, as well as new facts disclosed in Surah Baqarah. Lessons about drinking intoxicants, divorce, marriage, usury, menstruation, convincing proofs, punishment, and other subjects are revealed in Surah Al-Baqarah. Challenge yourself to change the things that you are doing that go against the teachings of the Qur'an and the Traditions and the Sunnah of the Prophet (s.a.w.s). In the Hadith of Sahih Al-Bukhari 50, Volume 1 Book 2 (Belief), Number 48 (English Reference) Narrated: Abu Huraira.

"One day while the Prophet (s.a.w.s) was sitting in the company of some people. (The Angel) Gabriel came and asked."

"What is faith?"

Allah's Apostle replied, "Faith is to believe in Allah, His angels, (the) meeting with Him, His Apostles, and to believe in Resurrection."

Then He further asked, *"What is Islam?"*

Allah's Apostle replied, "To worship Allah Alone and no one else, to offer prayers perfectly to pay the compulsory charity (Zakat), and to obey fasts during the month of Ramadan.

"Then He further asked, *"What is Ihsan (perfection)?"*

Allah's Apostle replied, "To worship Allah as if you see Him, and if you cannot achieve this state of devotion then you must consider that He is looking at you."

Then He further asked, *"When will the Hour be established?"*

Allah's Apostle replied, "The answer has no better knowledge than the questioner. But I will inform you about its portents." When a slave (Lady) gives birth to her master. When the shepherds of black camels start boasting and competing with others in the construction of higher buildings. And the Hour of one of five things which nobody knows except Allah."

Sahih Bukhari 50, Vol. 1, Book 2 (Belief), Hadith 48 (English Reference)

"The Prophet then recited; "Verily, with Allah (Alone,) is the knowledge of the Hour—"(31. 34). Then that man (Gabriel) left, and the Prophet asked his companions to call him back, but they could not see him. Then the Prophet said, (34)"That was Gabriel, who came to teach the people their faith" Abu 'Abdullah said He (The Prophet) considered all that as a part of faith."

As practicing "New Muslims", we must understand what Islam truly means; we must understand the spiritual daily obligation of having to make Salah five times per day on time as it is a great benefit that drives our steadfastness, strength, Mercy, and contentment in our earthly journey.

Moreover, it is a means of cleansing the soul of our sins we willingly or unwillingly committed throughout our earthly journeys. Remember that only Allah (s.w.t) alone knows when He will call us back to him from this world. Live your lives in the pious of ways for when Judgment Day comes you can at least say you have strived to live as Allah (s.w.t) instructed.

According to the Qur'an and the Sunnah of the Prophet (s.a.w.s) as reported in the Hadiths, and all His other scriptures of the past. Think about what you are looking for in this life, if it is anything other than Islam then you need to compare whatever it is to the Surah's and Ayah's of the Holy Qur'an.

Qur'an Ali-'Imran: 3: 83 asks this question.

"Are they looking for a faith other than the Deen (faith and way of life) of Allah knowing well that everything in the heavens and on the earth, willingly or unwillingly, has submitted to Him? And to Him, they shall all return."

There is nothing like that light bulb that turns on in your head when you are reading something, and you receive that divine message of truth. That is known as the spiritual inspiration at that moment when Allah (s.w.t) has chosen to reveal the secrets of the Qur'an when He opens up your crown chakra and downloads the message to your heart, now that is revelations for you, and we say, Alhamdul Allah.

CHAPTER SEVEN

LEARNING ABOUT ISLAM

It is the duty of every Muslim to learn about Islam and not just by listening to what other people, Muslim and non-Muslim alike have to say about it. Making every effort to learn how to draw a sound conclusion based on evidence from reliable sources. As a "New Muslim," you need to first, properly learn how to perform Salah, (prayer) you must then learn the correct recitation of the Qur'an in its original language of Arabic.

In 19 Countries around the world, the Arabic language is the major language used, and seven Countries speak dual languages with Arabic being the minor of the languages. There are more than 400 million people around the world speaking the Arabic language today coupled with various dialects of the language.

These are some of the reasons why it would be in your best interest to learn the language of the Qur'an so that you may remember Allah and the Surahs he revealed through memorization and also to communicate with the citizens of other countries that use Arabic as the preferred language of the people and the government.

During her travels, Asiah, a practicing Muslim, made it a priority, to learn basic languages for communication. She recommends you hire a teacher or take a Qur'anic class to improve your recitation of the Qur'anic Surahs.' You must be consistent with your study of Arabic because once you have mastered the Arabic Alphabet it is just a matter of time before you begin to read in Arabic and understand its meaning in your native dialect or language. Then you need to study and learn through authentic Hadith namely Sahih Bukhari and Muslim and the compilation of Hadith by Riyad-us-Saliheen which are most widely referenced in books.

Hadiths are a collection of reported sayings, deeds, and traditions about the behavior and the character of the Prophet (s.a.w.s), what he said, and his advice. These Hadiths are narrated reports about the life of Prophet Muhammad, s.a.w.s. (Ahmed, his given name by his mother) and how he led by an excellent example of how a Muslim should behave and treat other fellow human beings. As well as the type of character, a Muslim should strive to achieve in life when dealing with any of life's pleasures or mishaps.

Many Hadiths and the Qur'an have been translated into various other languages allowing others the opportunity to read the Qur'an and Hadiths in the language of their tongue, but it is recommended that you learn how to read and write the original language of the Qur'an, which is the Arabic. The knowledge of Fiqh (Islamic Jurisprudence), the understanding and application of Shari'ah enables you to do acts of worship properly agreed upon. Learn and study the fundamentals of your Islamic beliefs, search the life history of the early Muslims because it is the essential key piece for a "New Muslim" to learn. Do not restrict yourself or think that you can never become a scholar because there are many scholars today who were not born into Islam however their due diligence in study and research, they have made about Islam helped them to become outstanding scholars of the Deen (way of life or faith) Islam.

History reports that Muslims ruled Spain for eight hundred years until Christian Crusaders forced them out, and the Arabic language had been banned in Spain so long as the Christian Crusaders ruled. Then in Arabia, the British and the French ruled for a few years while the Muslims ruled Arabia for at least 1400 years. The largest amount of

Muslims around the world would be in Indonesia and Malaysia and on the East Coast of The Continent of Africa the spread of Islam has been enormous just like that of the United States according to the U.S. Census Bureau, America has a huge population of Muslims the estimation is about 5 to 8 million roughly, (1% to 2%) however it may as well be much more than reported because there are those Muslims who are not reporting their faith as being that of Islam. Therefore, it would be a bit difficult to determine the actual population of Muslims living in America.

Personal story, Asiah's ex-husband Usman has taught science for about 10 years in the African Country of Nigeria, and he was also a leader among the youth in his Country. With that said as a teacher he would advise the students and listen to the many different scholars who talk about and teach Islam. Make external efforts to seek clarity about the lectures. Ask for proof, in other words, evidence of the information spoken about. Start researching on your own about the evidence provided to you on the issues in Islam, and the traditions of the Prophet (s.a.w.s) written by the scholars. In doing so you will become a guided Muslim and a learned person about the important issues in Islam such as the wearing of a face veil for women.

As well as the issues of women having any choices or rights in Islam, obtaining knowledge about such issues will give you an advantage in teaching others about what you have learned about Islamic law, The Sunnah, and the behavior of a Muslim.

Understanding that women don't need to attend Jummah services, as it is of men in Islam. However, it has been reported, and Narrated by Salim Bin 'Abdullah, many times from various Hadith that the Prophet (s.a.w.s) clearly stated to the Muslim men of Islam should not stop their wives from attending Jummah services

Sahih Bukhari, Volume 1, Book 12, Number 832, pg.204, 2009)

> "If the wife of any of you asks for permission to go to the mosque, do not stop her from going to the mosque, although their houses are better for them"(Salim Bin 'Abdullah)

The Prophet (s.a.w.s) made this declaration because he was personally aware of the obligations facing married women who are raising children. Women were responsible for maintaining the household, caring for the children, and seeing to the everyday requirements of their husbands.

The Prophet (s.a.w.s) was inspired to cut short his prayers for the benefit of the mothers of the children present at the Jummah services by the fact that ladies who visited the mosque with their children would frequently weep because they required the attention of their parents. Women should participate in the *Eid-ul-Fitra and Eid-ul-Adha* celebrations rather than choose between going to prayer services or staying at home.

The Prophet Muhammad, s.a.w.s., is not advocating that women should not attend Jummah prayers; rather, He is urging mothers of young children to join in on the holiday celebrations because it would be easier for them to do rather than stand for Jummah prayers, with her crying child that may cause an issue among the ummah (community).

The crying child also prevents the Prophet from having longer prayer time thus causing the Prophet to take pity and shorten the prayers and the crying child will also disturb the prayers and worship of others to Allah (s.w.t.).

(Sahih Bukhari, Volume 1, Book 12, Number 827, pg.203, 2009), Narrated 'Abdullah bin Abi Qatad al-Ansari:

> "My father said, "Allah's Apostle said, whenever I stand for prayer, I want to prolong it but on hearing the cries of a child I would shorten it as I disliked putting its mother in trouble."

The Prophet (s.a.w.s) received revelations from Allah (s.w.t) telling him that the practice of burying newborn females alive had to stop. Before Allah (God), both men and women are equal. Women received divinely sanctioned inheritance, property, social, and marriage rights, including the ability to request a divorce and reject a proposal's stipulations. As you can see, it would be quite beneficial for you to learn about the actual traditions and Sunnah of Islam. Because other Islamic nations have developed the practice of fusing their cultural practices with Islamic tradition, which the Qur'an and hadiths forbid. The beliefs, habits, acts, and so on of a specific civilization, group, area, or period make up culture, as defined by the Merriam-Webster Dictionary. Islam opposes any cultural practices or notions that go against its principles and strategies.

For instance, the Imam of Dakar, Senegal, Africa informed Asiah's present husband, Ibrahim, that we could not be married until after Maghrib prayer while Asiah was organizing their Nikah (wedding). This was untrue; the customs and traditions were those of the African Senegalese people, not those of Islam or the Sunnah and Traditions of Islam.

The attitude of the unbelievers recorded in the Qur'an, who rejected Islam because they preferred what their ancestors did before them, is comparable to accepting cultural concepts that conflict with Islam.

Qur'an Surah Baqarah (2 : 170)

> "And when it is said to them, "follow what Allah has revealed, "they say, "Rather, we will follow that which we found our fathers doing." Even though their fathers were idol worshipers and had no true guidance or understanding of the Almighty Allah (s.w.t) revealed to the Prophet Muhammad, (s.a.w.s.) for all of mankind.

Understanding the principles of your faith, Islam is essential for strengthening your identity as a devoted Muslim. Proficiency in performing prayers accurately not only enriches your spiritual life but also positions you as a proponent of the authentic practices of Islam, following the Sunnah of the Prophet (peace be upon him).Moreover, a comprehensive grasp of the Arabic language in the Qur'an empowers you to translate its profound teachings into your mother tongue, fostering a deeper connection to the scriptures.

CHAPTER EIGHT

PREPARING FOR SALAT

Qur'an Al-Ma'idah 5: [6]

(6) "O believers! When you rise for Salah (prayer), wash your face and your hands as far as the elbows, wipe your head with wet hands, and wash your feet to the ankles. If you have an emission of semen, then take a full bath. However, if you are sick, or on a journey, or you have used the toilet, or you had intercourse with your women (your wives) and you do not find any water then resort to Tayammum – fine clean soil and rub your faces and hands with it. Allah does not wish to burden you; He favors upon you so that you may be thankful."

The literal translation for Salat is prayer, one of the most important acts of worship in Islam, and as a Muslim. It is the second Pillar of Islam you will be accountable for on the judgment day because Salah is the second (Obligatory act of worship to Allah), and the first is Tawheed declaring your "(Oneness of Allah)" However many of us who are Muslim feel lazy to perform Salat, some Muslims' incorrectly perform Salat.

Once we make ablution, we should stay away from anything that can invalidate our ablution or anything and anyone that will cause distraction between us, and our Rabb during our time of performing Salat (prayer). In our preparation for Salah (prayer) as Muslims, we must first perform ablution, which is the cleansing of our entire body, or wudu the cleaning of certain parts of our body. Now you are ready for your daily Salah (prayer). Remember the act of ablution or wudu must be performed each time you intend to perform Salah (prayer). Unless you are already in the Musallah (place of worship, Masjid) awaiting your prayer time, provided you have not (pass gas) or any nullifying issues that would violate your ablution.

Now on the other side of preparing for Salah (prayer), it is "Haram" for any believing Muslim to offer Salah (prayer) when one has consumed an alcoholic beverage for the lack of a clear understanding of what they are saying in prayer to Allah (s.w.t.) while in their state of drunkenness. A believing Muslim should not offer Salah (prayer) after having sexual intercourse with a woman (wife), or man (husband) until you perform Ghusl Janabah, washing of the entire body.

A believing Muslim should not offer Salah (prayer) if they are in a state of Major impurity or minor impurity and while Menstruating (women). You also must not touch the Qur'an which is not lawful for someone in a state of Major impurity or Menstruating, such as the release of body urine, emesis, blood, or fesses. However, there are specific instructions within the Qur'an that explain the reasons why one should perform Tayammum by using the clean soil of the earth and rubbing your face and hands with it when one is traveling and unable to find water. Here are some of the reasons.

- ❖ If you are sick or on a journey
- ❖ If any of the travelers have used the toilet
- ❖ If you have had contact with women (sexual relations with wives)

These acts are done only if you are unable to find water to wash your body after these particular functions. One of the most important conditions of worship is ablution (The Ablution—Al Wuduw'u) and that is by way of purification from impurity.

Qur'an An-Nisa 4: [43]

(43) "O believers! Do not offer Salah (prayer) when you are drunk until you can understand what you are saying, nor after seminal emission except when you are traveling unless you wash your whole body. If you are sick, or on a journey, or one of you has used the toilet, or has had contact with women (sexual relation with wives) and can find no water, then make Tayammum: take some clean earth and rub your faces and hands with it. Allah is Oft-Pardoning, Oft-Forgiving."

Now, please don't think that this ayah of the Qur'an is giving any Muslim permission to become intoxicated so long as you are not praying because it is not, in another Surah of the Qur'an there is an ayah that further expounds on the intoxication for drinking alcohol, that advises you to abstain from drinking and gambling in part.

[Qur'an Al-Ma'idah: 5(91-92)]

(91) "...Shaitan desires to stir up enmity and hatred between you with intoxicants and gambling, to prevent you from the remembrance of Allah and Salah (prayers). Will you not abstain?" (92) "Obey Allah and obey the Rasool and abstain from these things. If you do not, then you should know that our Rasool's' duty is only to convey My **message clearly...**"

Preparing for Salah (prayer) is an important part of the daily activities of a practicing Muslim (male) and Muslimah (female). As the Prophet Muhammad, s.a.w.s. (Ahmed, his given name by his mother) said, he who seeks knowledge Allah will prepare a place for them in paradise, as a Muslim it is our "duty to seek this knowledge" (Bukhari) until our last breath of air. Even Allah (s.a.w.s) speaks about knowledge in terms of Taqwa, one who is (Ilah) God, consciousness, piousness, and has fear of Allah, love for Allah, and self-restraint.

Qur'an Surah Al-Fatir (35 : 28) reads.

(28) "Those of His servants only who are possessed of knowledge fear Allah surely Allah is Mighty, Forgiving."

Therefore, any Muslim also must prostrate five times daily the second activity of the 'Five Pillars' Salah (prayer). We are all victims of misperceptions and prejudice at one time or another in our lives. But when you are a victim, you must find a way to sort things out and find your way to set the record straight in this case through Salah (prayer) all things are made possible when you remember Allah (s.w.t), before you do something that is not displaying the true character of a Muslim or the Sunnah of the Prophet Muhammad, s.a.w.s.(Ahamed, his given name by his mother). There is also a Hadith narrated by 'Abdullah ibn Mas'ud (R.A.A) that said he asked the Messenger of Allah (p.b.u.h)

"What deed is most beloved by Allah?" (s.w.t) he said,

"To offer each prayer as soon as it is due." He then asked him again "Then what?" He said, "Treating one's parents with mercy and respect. Yet again, he asked him, "Then what?" He said, "Jihad (fighting) for the sake of Allah (s.w.t)."

There are "Five Pillars in Islam" for Muslims to adhere to but of the five the two most important should be your declaration to Allah (s.w.t) and praising Him when you are making Salah (prayer) five times daily as you ask that He forgive your sins. Even the Prophet Muhammad, s.a.w.s.(Ahamed, his given name by his mother) knew of the importance of prostrating in Salah (prayer) for the praising of Allah (s.w.t) because it is only through the Mercy, Grace, and Blessings of our Creator that we are living in this Dunya (world). Amin!

<u>The Five Obligatory Worships Are:</u>

1. Salaatul Fajr (Morning Worship)—*Two (2) raka'aat.* It's time from dawn (a light not followed by darkness) till the sun appears on the horizon.

2. *Salaatudh Dhur (Early Afternoon Worship)—Four (4) raka'aat.* Its time is when the sun surpasses the Meridian until the shade of every object becomes equal to it in addition to the shade caused by the sun in the position of the Meridian.

3. *Salaatul 'Asr (Late Afternoon Worship)-* It consists of, four *(4) raka'aat.* Its time is from after every object's shade becomes equal to it in addition to the shade caused by the sun in the position of the Meridian until sunset.

4. *Salaatul Maghrib (Sunset Worship)-*It consists of *three (3) raka'aat.* It's time when the sun appears to set on the horizon until there is the appearance of the redness of the twilight,

5. *Salaatul 'Ishaa (Late Evening Worship)*-It constitutes *four (4) raka'aat.* Its time is from the disappearance of the redness of the twilight to midnight.

<u>The Elements (Arkan) of Salat prayer are five:</u>

- ❖ Intention (Niyyat)
- ❖ Takbiratul Ehram
- ❖ Qiyam (Standing before the Ruku, if able)
- ❖ Ruku (Bowing as you touch your knees)
- ❖ Sajdah, Sitting, and Bowing forehead to the floor (Two prostrations in every Rak'at)

The obligatory acts of payers meaning the position a Muslim must perform are elemental i.e., primary, or basic (Intention, Takbiratul, Qiyam, Ruku, and Sajdah).

Therefore, if you forget the position of Salah (prayer), and you remember it then you should correctly submit your prayer to Allah because you would like Allah to accept all of your prayers. The position of prayer and the time you offer the prayers are of significant importance, why else would Allah (s.w.t) send the Angel (Gabriel) to demonstrate to the Prophet Muhammad, s.a.w.s.(Ahmed, his given name by his mother) how to perform the Salah (prayer) and at what times of the day.

In Volume 1, Book 10, Number 500; narrated by Ibn Shihab, Hadith in part."
(Sahih Bukhari, 2009, pg.130)

> "Once 'Umar bin 'Abdul 'Aziz delayed the prayer and 'Urwa bin Az-Zubair went to him and said, "Once in 'Iraq, Al MughTra bin Shu'ba delayed his prayers and Abi Mas'ud Al-Ansari went to him and said 'O Mughra' what is this? Don't you know that once Gabriel came and offered the prayer (Fajr prayer) and Allah's Apostle prayed too..."Gabriel said I was ordered to demonstrate the prayers prescribed to you.

As a Muslim, it is essential to ensure that you are performing Salah (prayers) in the correct positions at the prescribed times. The act of praying is a fundamental pillar of Islam, and it is crucial to fulfill the criteria set by Allah (s.w.t) for the acceptance of our prayers.

Moreover, when attending Friday's Jummah prayer services, it is important to show respect by switching off cell phones. Additionally, if you have children with you, it's important to ensure that they do not disrupt other members of the Masjid during prayer times. This will help to maintain the solemnity and focus of the congregational prayer

CHAPTER NINE

PROPAGATING ISLAM

It is a misconception to say only scholars are eligible to preach about Islam. Various levels of Muslims can preach about Islam. For example, calling a friend for Salah (prayer) is a way to propagate Islam. You do not need the title of a scholar to preach or teach Islam because this is a duty placed upon every Muslim. Likewise forbidding evil does not require the highest level of knowledge to make someone aware that what they are doing is incorrect according to Allah (s.w.t.) the Qur'an, Sunnah, and moral behavior.

As a "New Muslim", people will come to you and wonder what called you to Islam and why you decided to become a Muslim. There is no need to shy away from them, just tell them your story if you choose to. Explain to them the good things you have seen in Islam through someone who has exemplified the character of a model Muslim. Don't be afraid to talk about the literature you have read or videos you listened to, explain to them how your life has changed for the better since you have become a Muslim and embraced Islam. Perhaps your story could be enough to prompt them into researching on their own, about the Deen (way of life or faith) of Islam and its history.

The best way to call people to Islam is through your actions and your character. People are always observant of other people, especially in the workplace, in their community, and their family's paternal (father's side) and maternal (mother's side). In their observation of you, they begin to wonder if the actual teaching of Islam brings about curiosity for them.

Once you put what you have learned about the behaviors of a practicing Muslim into motion, whether you understand it or not, you have just begun propagating about Islam. In other words, your action speaks loud and clear to all those who are observing you. With so many immoral acts, going on in this society today you may find it difficult to propagate the Deen (way of life or faith) of Islam to others because of the disdain most of society has for Muslims in light of the acts of terror against the innocent men, women, and children of all nationalities that include Muslims. With a little effort, you can preach about Islam by showing people a comparison to their Religious faith by using the Torah (The Five Books of Musa), Injeel (The Gospel of Matthew, Mark, Luke, and John, about Isa/Jesus) in comparison to The Holy Qur'an (A Compilation of Revelations received by Prophet Muhammad, s.a.w.s.(Ahmed, his given name by his mother) for all of mankind.

Using these three books will help you find ways of showing the commonalities in your Faiths and theirs.

In The Qur'an Surah Al-Baqarah (2: 137) says,

(137) "So, if they believe (accept Islam) like you have believed they shall be rightly guided, if they reject it, they will surely fall into dissension (divide into differing factions); Allah will be your sufficient defender against them, and He hears and knows everything."

The gross misinformation about Islam and Muslims through media hype that leads to discrimination and acts of violence against Muslims may shut you down from the propagation of Islam for fear of assault by those who do not understand the true peace that Islam teaches or preaches.

True fundamentalist of Islam adheres to the true doctrine or the ideology of the Qur'an, and Sunnah that has given Muslims a system of beliefs through The Holy Qur'an that are truly the words of Allah (s.w.t) and not that of the Prophet (s.a.w.s).

The Hadiths are a set of Books written in volumes about the traditions, character, and sayings of the Prophet (s.a.w.s) as narrated and reported by the Sahaabah (Companions), family members, and the works of some very famous Scholars who have lived in the error of the Prophet (s.a.w.s). A true Muslim should only follow The Glorious Qur'an because this Book holds the laws, the words of prevention, and a guide on how to walk the righteous straight path in life.

The Sunnah of the Prophet Muhammad, s.a.w.s (Ahmed, given name by his mother) that are written in a set of Books known as the Sahih Hadith an added advantage because it gives a narrative account of the traditions, characters, and sayings of the Prophet (s.a.w.s). Muslims can agree with the views of any scholar as long as they confirm the teachings of the Qur'an, (*the* commandments of Allah, (s.w.t) and Sunnah (the actions, sayings, and practice of the Prophet, s.a.w.s). If such views go against the work of Allah, or the Sunnah of His Prophet (s.a.w.s), then they carry no weight, regardless of how learned the scholar might be. Surah An-Nisa talks about standing for justice despite yourself and others around you.

Qur'an An-Nisa (4: 135, pg. 206)

[135] "O believers stand firm for justice and bear true witness for the sake of Allah, even though it be against yourselves, your parents, or your relatives. It does not matter whether the party is rich or poor, Allah is the well-wisher of both. So let not your selfish desires swerve you from justice. If you distort your

testimony or decline to give it, then you should remember that
Allah is fully aware of your actions."

"Humanity must remember that we cannot hide anything from Allah (s.w.t) because 'He' knows everything we know and everything we do, Therefore, as a Muslim, when you are out there spreading Islam, please do not alter your testimony or refuse to share it with anyone, as your story may save another person's life. The information above lets you know that regardless of how learned the Scholar might be, you as a Muslim must only follow the Qur'an and the Sunnah (the actions, sayings and practice of His Prophet, s.a.w.s) because if the Scholars or the Sahih Hadith is in discrepancy with the Qur'an then, hands down you must follow what Qur'an says after all it is the true hadith and revelation revealed to the Prophet, (s.a.w.s) through the angel Gabriel with the permission of Allah (s.w.t).

Remember that when you begin to preach about Islam and others begin to speak badly about Islam, please do not get into an argument with them just walk away and try to reach them another day through a different medium, this would be best for you and the Deen of Islam.

Qur'an Surah An-Nisa (4: 140, pg. 206) Reads.

> [140] "He has already revealed for you in the Book that when you hear Allah's revelations being denied or ridiculed by people, you must not sit with them unless they change the topic of their talk, otherwise you shall be considered guilty like them. Rest assured that Allah is going to gather the hypocrites and the unbelievers all together in hell."

As a new Muslim or an existing member of the Muslim community, it's important to remember that when others speak negatively about Islam, it's not productive to participate in conversations that bash our religion.

Engaging in such discussions can be viewed as hypocritical and not in line with the principles of Islam. Instead, it's crucial to represent our faith in a positive light and to approach these discussions with understanding and patience.

In our efforts to educate and share our beliefs, it's important to engage in open dialogues with people from diverse backgrounds. Many individuals are interested in learning about the history and practices of Muslims, and it's an opportunity for us to address misconceptions and stereotypes. By doing so, we can foster greater understanding and mutual respect. Furthermore, it's important to engage in these conversations with humility and empathy, especially when discussing the Prophet Isa (Jesus, peace be upon him). We should be mindful of the differing beliefs and perspectives of others and strive to convey our own beliefs respectfully. Many people often wonder why we use the term Allah (s.w.t) instead of simply saying "God." It's important to understand that Allah is simply the Arabic word for God (illa/illah). Just as every language has its unique name for the concept of a higher power, Arabic uses Allah to refer to the divine being. For example, in Greek, the word for God is Theos, and in Hebrew, God is referred to as Elohim, Yahuwah, or YHWH, which translates to "the Lord God." It's fascinating to note that Arabic is a Semitic language, sharing its roots with Hebrew and Aramaic, the language spoken by Jesus (a.s.). As a result, the Arabic word for God, Allah, shows remarkable similarity to the names used for God in these other Semitic languages.

We choose to use the name Allah because it represents the breath of life that every human being and animal inhales. For those who believe, the attributes of Allah (s.w.t) provide significant protection and blessings.

In The Quran Surah Al-Hashr (59: 24) says,

(59) "He is Allah, The Creator, The Inventor, The Fashioner; To Him belong the best names."

In response to the curiosity of non-Muslims, it is important to clarify that within Islam, women do have the option to not wear the hijab (head covering) or the veil (facial covering). Additionally, there is concern about whether Muslim women are oppressed by their faith or by their husbands, and whether they have rights as women in Islam. It is crucial to note that before the advent of Islam, women were indeed mistreated, and infant baby girls were tragically buried alive. However, with the arrival of Prophet Muhammad (peace be upon him), revelations on the rights of women were sent, heralding a new era of respect and equality. In Islam, the position of women is considered to be like that of men, as both have their own set of rights bestowed upon them by Allah through the Prophet (s.a.w.s). However, there is a distinction in the responsibilities assigned to each gender. Men are considered one degree above women in terms of responsibility, as they are seen as the providers and protectors of their families. On the other hand, within the home, women are regarded as the rulers. It's important to note that absolute equality between men and women does not exist, except in the sight of Allah. This is evident in various aspects such as childbirth, marriage, and physical strength, where differences exist and are recognized within Islamic teachings.

It is beneficial to familiarize yourself with the life of a Muslim by delving into the texts such as the Qur'an, and Sahih Hadith, and learning about the Sunnah of Prophet Muhammad, peace be upon him, who advocated for the rights of women in Islam and fought against oppression. Understanding the "Five Pillars of Islam" and "The Articles of Faith" can provide valuable insights when discussing Islam with others.

In The Qur'an Surah Al-Baqarah (2: 228, pg.145) Reads.

[145] "...Women have rights, similar to those equitably exercised against them, although men have a status (degree of responsibility) above them. Allah is Mighty, Wise."

As the person inquiring approaches you, they will perceive you as a knowledgeable Muslim who deeply comprehends and embraces their faith. Your exemplary character, piety, and conduct will gradually guide them, providing them with the opportunity to seek knowledge through the book references you've carefully selected and the way you present the information.

True Islam serves as a guiding light for those who are lost, helping them navigate through life's challenges. A devout Muslim imparts the wisdom of how to shield oneself with the words of Allah against the temptations of Shaytan (the cursed one), without distorting the truth to attract others to our faith. A sincere believer, living with Taqwa (God-consciousness) every day, enables the seeker of knowledge to genuinely explore and determine if Islam truly aligns with their way of life and faith.

In The Qur'an Surah An-Nisa (4: 60) says this about Shaytan,

(60) "Have you not seen those who claim that they believe in what has been revealed to you and other prophets before you? Yet, they desire that the Judgment (in their disputes) be made by Taghoot (Kafir Laws-Shaytan) though they were commanded to reject them, and Shaytan's wish is to lead them far astray into deep error."

As Muslims, whether you are new to the faith or have been practicing for a while, spreading the message of Islam is one of our fundamental responsibilities. Our duty is to guide those who may not comprehend the true essence of the natural way of life, Al-Islam, without distorting the truth, even when it may be challenging. It is crucial to remember that Shaytan, the sworn enemy of humanity, is determined to lead people astray and away from the teachings of Allah (s.w.t). A similar struggle is exemplified in the story of Isa ibn Maryam

(Jesus), who, facing the temptations of Shaytan (c.h), steadfastly adhered to the commandments of Allah Ta'ala, triumphing over Shaytan's attempts to deceive him.

Satan (c.h.) was beaten back by Isa/Jesus saying.

(Matthew 4: 4,9-11)

> [4] "Then was Jesus led up of the spirit into the wilderness to be tempted of the devil." [9] And said unto him, all these things will I give you, if you will fall and worship me." [10] "Then said Jesus unto him, Get thee hence, Satan: for it is written, You should worship the Lord God, and Him only should you serve." [11] Then the devil left him, and behold, angels came and ministered unto him."
>
> [23] "And then I will profess unto them, I never knew you: depart from me, you that work iniquity."

He Isa/Jesus (a.s.) is known for his unwavering commitment to Salah (prayer), demonstrating his dedication to spiritual connection and mindfulness. Similarly, the Prophet Muhammad (s.a.w.s) upheld a profound reverence for the Qur'an, exemplifying the qualities of a peaceful and trustworthy Muslim through his remembrance of Allah during prayer and in his everyday actions.

As a new Muslim or someone who has been practicing Islam for many years, it can be challenging when we fall short of fulfilling the obligatory five prayers per day. However, it's important to remember that even in moments of struggle, holding on to the rope of Allah, seeking forgiveness, and asking for continued guidance is crucial as we progress in our Islamic journey. Allah is ever-forgiving, and as Muslims, we believe that seeking forgiveness is a way to cleanse ourselves and draw closer to Allah's mercy and guidance. Additionally, in our prayers and the propagation of Islam, we should strive to embody the exemplary characteristics of Prophet Muhammad and Isa (Jesus) and always keep the remembrance of Allah in our hearts and actions.

CHAPTER TEN

OBSTACLES AND CHALLENGES

One cannot achieve success without going through certain obstacles and challenges in this life. Shaytan (the devil, c.h) is never happy when he loses one of his followers. He Shaytan (c.h) will make a continuous effort to take back the souls of every believing Muslim if he can. New Muslims need to understand that many things will come your way as a testament to your faith in Allah (s.w.t). You need to hold on to the rope of Allah (s.w.t) and surround yourself with the most pious of Muslims who have the best of intentions because no matter how strong your faith may be Allah will surely test you in your Deen ((way of life or faith).

Allah, states in the Qur'an Surah Al-Baqarah (2: 214)

(214) "Do you think that you will enter Paradise without any trials while you have known the examples of those who passed away before you? They were afflicted with suffering and adversity and were so violently shaken up that even the Rasuul

and the believers with him cried out: "When will Allah's help come?" Be aware! Allah's help is ever close.

People face different challenges as "New Muslims," it would appear as though your challenges and obstacles escalate to levels you are not able to get through once you have become a Muslim. You need to continue being steadfast in your walk toward righteousness. Embrace yourselves for the situations you will face in this life from family, friends, husbands, wives, and unknown forces Be wary of any obstacles or challenges thrown your way by Shaytan (jinn) and his followers. Is nothing less than what earlier Muslims faced when they chose to follow the words revealed to the Prophet Muhammad (s.a.w.s.) by the angel Gabriel. Giving the Prophet a comprehensive set of instructions on how we should live and act.

The Prophet (a.s.) received these revelations at different periods of his life. The Ayahs and Surahs are recorded in the Noble Holy Qur'an. It would do all "New Muslim," a great deed to read about the history of the earlier Muslims and the ways they were able to overcome the obstacles and challenges, faced for the cause of Islam and the fight for freedom and their rights as a people. Nevertheless, the earlier Muslims persevered giving them a stronger righteous commitment to Islam and their Iman (faith). It taught them how to deal with and overcome these obstacles and challenges through the daily five prayers, and the knowledge that Allah (s.w.t) would give them what they needed to survive these obstacles and challenges as they hold on to their Iman (faith). Insha Allah (if Allah will). Every new and older Muslim will be faced with Obstacles and Challenges at some point in their lives. These Obstacles and Challenges are for those who were born into Deen-ul Islam and those who were chosen for Deen-ul Islam. Parents will present challenges since they frequently believe that their way of doing things in this world is ideal, treating you as if you don't have an opinion or anything resembling your thoughts.

You can now accept and believe that, because they shared comparable experiences as children, our parents do indeed possess the ability to see and predict what will happen when we make particular decisions in our lives as children and adults. When teachers instruct you about the history of Islam in a classroom, the majority of whom are not Muslims, they do so in a way that leaves you feeling uncertain about your Iman (faith). They also ask you to research the material they have presented to you. Family members who follow a different religion feel the need to disprove your choice of faith because you chose to become Muslim rather than staying within the confines of Judaism, Christianity, or any other religious faith. An employer who wants you to believe that the Islamic faith is not the best for you to practice because they hold your financial livelihood in their pockets as the employer enquires about why you chose Islam or whether you were born a Muslim. Friends who have been labeled as outcasts and shunned have chosen not to dress in Muslim garb because it makes them blend in with the rest of society. Their decisions were influenced by people inside and outside of their homes. Then there is communal life; whether you live in a completely Islamic setting or a mixed community, the likelihood that your family will deal with addiction and unreliable friends is the chance we take when our community is mixed with the righteous and the unrighteous people of the Dunya (world).

Asiah lived in an Islamic environment for eight months in the country of Qatar which gave her a sense of peace and tranquility that she had not experienced in America. When she traveled to Ghana and Senegal of Africa, it gave her the same sense of peace and tranquility living among Muslims and Christians side by side in harmony. Wow! Such a wonderful sensation. Now, in no way is Asiah attempting to imply that these nations do not have their difficulties or flaws because they do. It was just comforting to know that she wasn't being judged for choosing to convert to Islam and adopt it as her Deen (way of life). In these difficult times, your family would prefer that you not convert to Islam. Parents insist that you surround yourself only with those who share your beliefs and practice the same Iman (faith), yet this may or may not help you to remain steadfast in your Ibadah (worship), no matter your religious choice. In Asiah's personal experience, she has found that a child's upbringing greatly influences their path in life. This is especially true for children who are born into the Islamic faith and face persecution for their beliefs during their formative years. As they reach adulthood, some of these children may choose to distance themselves from their faith. Asiah's eldest son, for instance, faced life-threatening danger due to his Muslim heritage, which he inherited at birth. The same is true for his siblings. It's important to remember the following text:

Growing up as a child, it can be difficult to come to terms with the fact that Islam was not a personal choice, but rather the faith chosen by parents at birth. This situation presents significant challenges for both parents and children, as they strive to navigate and overcome obstacles. One such obstacle involves finding ways to protect oneself from those who fail to comprehend the true essence of Islam. This miscomprehension often stems from the actions of a small number of individuals who claim to be practicing Muslims yet tarnish the faith through their destructive behavior. Furthermore, some individuals perpetrate heinous acts and falsely attribute their actions to divine instruction, causing immense suffering to innocent men, women, and children. This is not what true Islam is about we come to you in peace until you make the conscious decision to harm our family and only then shall we defend ourselves as Allah (s.w.t) so instructed that of the Prophet Muhammad, (s.a.w.s.) to fight against the oppressor and persecutors of innocent men, women and infant baby girls, and for the right to have an abode (home) in the City of their birth homeland of which the earlier Muslims were thrown out of.

> ➤ *Obstacles and Challenges as Parents:*

Parents often like their children to fall in line with what they are doing or practicing as a faith. Most parents don't always welcome their children's stance on changing their faith from what the family is practicing. They see their children as leaving their Deen (way of life or faith) of Islam as an insult and a slap to the face of the family. Some parents disown the child and cast them out of the family, denying them any inheritance from the family. Do not feel bad if you come from a wealthy family and you are cast out. Mushab bin Umar came from a wealthy family and attempts by his mother to deny him wealth and bring him back to kufr (disbelief) only increased his guidance into the light of Islam.

Although he died as a poor man, he was among those who had certainty of paradise. The paradise that Allah (s.w.t) promised is far better and everlasting than whatever you lost because of accepting Islam. Some parents also go to the extreme of beating their children, insulting them, and causing public embarrassment. If you fall into this category, endure, and know that the verbal, physical, or mental beating from your parents could never compare with the beating of the Angels but this does not mean you have to allow your parents to abuse you. Take the matter up with an Imam (Islamic Leader) who will be honest in helping you, if not seek assistance from the legal authorities. However, some parents are less concerned about what faith their child chooses to practice my mother was truly one of those parents, she at first was taken aback but once I showed her my reasons, she stepped up to help me accomplish my mission of becoming a successful Muslim.

On the day that Allah (s.w.t) guided Asiah to accept Islam, she felt a great deal of anxiety because she knew she had to inform her parents. With the help of Allah (s.w.t), Asiah was able to overcome this challenge by turning to the Torah sent through Moses, specifically the (Book of Leviticus 11:7-8), as her guide. This was the same Bible her mother, had studied as a Baptist Christian and the one she had used to raise Asiah and her siblings. She believed that by helping her parents understand her choice to embrace Islam, she might also encourage them to consider becoming Muslim. This was a significant and rewarding task, and she prayed for Allah (s.w.t) to make it easier for her. In most cases, parents do not like to listen to their children on the subject matter of faith. The prevailing belief is that religious guidance should flow from parents to children, rather than the other way around. Individual Muslims need to engage in conversations with their parents to convey the peaceful nature of Islam and its role as a way of life.

By doing so, they aim to demonstrate that they are not imposing their beliefs on their parents, but rather seeking to educate them about the principles of Islam and how it fosters peace within the family. This approach serves to avoid making parents feel as though their children are assuming the role of providers and instructors within the household.

> ## Obstacles and Challenges as a Father and as a Mother:

The father is the head of the family, the provider, and protector of his entire family. The mother is the nurturer of the children, the maintainer of the house and she takes care of the needs of her husband. When a child becomes the only one who has accepted Islam as their new Deen (way of life or faith) you can rest assured they will face many challenges. If you are a young man or woman who embraced Islam, you may go to your mother or perhaps your father for assistance. In doing so you must choose the parents that would help you succeed in the practice of your new Deen (way of life or faith). Perhaps your mother would be the one to help you to convince your father as to the reasons you reverted to Islam as a chosen faith, or it may turn out that your father can convince your mother seeing as he is the head of the family for Asiah it was her mother, she chose to inform about wanting to become a practicing Muslim.

As the head of the family and main provider, you might feel entitled to close your ears to your wife or child's reasoning. However, it's important to remember that being forceful will only exacerbate the situation. This could lead to your son persuading your wife to see reason, eventually resulting in her decision to embrace Islam as her faith. The situation of a wife who has newly embraced Islam while her husband has not can be challenging, especially when she begins to challenge her husband and make life at home uncomfortable. It's important to handle this situation with patience and understanding. Instead of resorting to extreme measures like divorce, it's crucial to fulfill your responsibilities as a father and maintain love for your family. Respecting your wife's decisions and maintaining a peaceful atmosphere at home is essential. It's advisable not to use force or coercion to enforce religious beliefs.

Rather, kindness and prayers can create a more harmonious environment. It's important to understand that children often have a strong bond with their mothers, and it's crucial to navigate these challenging situations with compassion and wisdom. As the central figure in the family, the father plays a crucial role in protecting and providing for his loved ones. Both parents need to engage in open and empathetic communication with their children regarding their decision to embrace Islam.

The husband, as the head of the household, should take the initiative to educate himself about the principles of the faith to better understand and support his wife and child. This is reminiscent of the contrast between the tyrannical nature of Pharaoh and the exemplary piety of his wife, Asiya bint Muzahim, who is revered by Muslims for her righteousness and faith.

In The Holy Qur'an Allah (s.w.t) speaks very highly of Asiya. In Surah Al-Tahrim (66: 11)

> [11] "And for the believers Allah has set an example in the wife of Fir'aun (Pharaoh), who said: "My Rabb! Build for me a house as a special favor from you in paradise, deliver me from Fir'aun and his misdeeds, and save me from the wicked nation."

Asiya accepted the Iman (faith) of the Prophet Musa (p.b.u.h) despite the evil ways of her husband, Pharaoh the tyrant. He made many attempts to persuade her to denounce the faith of Prophet Musa (p.b.u.h). He even sought the help of Asiya's mother she refused to reject the Iman (faith) of Musa (p.b.u.h) and because of this he tortured and murdered her as he had done other women of the same faith, (Islam). Therefore, you can understand just because you are the husband and the head of the house does not give you the right to decide which Iman (faith) your family should follow when, it has already been determined by Allah, (s.w.t) what we shall serve.

Our final determination will come in the hereafter and Allah will tell us if we are practicing the correct Deen (way of life or faith) so don't allow anyone to sway you from the ways of Allah (Ta'ala), the 'Five Pillars of Islam' and the 'Articles of Faith.' Study often, relax, and enjoy what you are learning remember that all experiences will not be good ones but for the most part, Asiah can say she loves being a Muslimah in Al-Islam.

In Islam, women have the right to divorce their husbands based on religious differences. However, Islam does not recommend it, nor does it suggest that a Muslim woman marry a non-Muslim man. This is because the woman is usually responsible for raising the children, and if there are children from a previous marriage who were raised in the Islamic faith, she should marry within Islam. This is because the Muslim husband has the right for his children to be raised in the Islamic faith, and this is his right as a Muslim man with children from a divorced Muslim wife. As for the child who has accepted Islam as their new Deen (way of life or faith) you need to know that Allah (s.w.t) has sent revelations to the Prophet Muhammad, s.a.w.s. (Ahmed, his given name by his mother) on how to handle the unbelievers he said, in Surah 68 Ayah' 51-52, 48:

Qur'an Surah 68: ayahs 51-52, 48.

[51] "The unbelievers would almost trip you up with their eyes when they hear our revelations (the Qur'an) and say: "He (Muhammad) is surely crazy." [52] "But this (the Qur'an) is nothing else than a Reminder to all the people of the world."

> (48) "So, wait with patience for the judgment of your Rabb and be not like the companion of the fish, who cried when he was in distress."

Referring to the Prophet Jonah, whom Allah (s.w.t) saved and included among the righteous, Asiahs advises you as a "New Muslim" to persevere with patience through obstacles and challenges you may face while propagating Islam. It is important to avoid suffering and affliction caused by impatience. By practicing patience, Allah will make things easy for you, just as He has made the Qur'an easy to remember, as long as we remember Allah.

Qur'an Surah Al-Qamar: (54: 17, pg.707-8)

> (17) "And we have indeed made the Qur'an very easy to understand and remember, so is there any who will remember?"

➤ *Obstacles and Challenges Old Habits:*

It has been said that old habits die hard! Many a time we become addicted to bad habits and immoral acts. There are several ways, we can move away from old habits, which are not a part of Islam. To deal with these old habits, you need to first, prostrate before Allah (s.w.t) asking His forgiveness each time you indulge in those bad habits. Ask Allah (s.w.t) to take away all urges of *"Haraam"* behaviors after which you begin your practical steps. Find alternative *"Halaal"* behaviors that can substitute for your bad habits. Staying away from bad company and people who continue to indulge in these bad habits you have because all bad habits have their consequences. Most times knowing the effects of your bad habits can help to move you away from them.

For instance, knowing that smoking cigarettes is bad for breathing and the health of those around you, the harmful effects of smoking are written on the side of the package. Do not wait for your bad habits to cause serious illness or health issues and then you decide to quit. In Islam, many things are, *"Halaal" and "Haraam"* which you can find in Surah: 2 Al-Baqarah. Finding better alternatives for your everyday bad habits *(Haraam)*, with everyday good habits *(Halaal)* is not all difficult you as a new Muslim are required to walk your path of righteousness one day at a time. Be aware of those practicing Muslims who will only tell you that something is *"Haraam"* but are unable to give you an alternative *"Halaal"* solution to your issue. It is your duty as a Muslim to ask for or to look for that *"Halaal"* alternative to your *"Haraam"* habits or behavior. Pray to Allah (s.w.t) for the strength to give up those bad habits and to bring you closer to Him. Take for example; simple fruit juices are an alternative to alcohol, they give you the much-needed vitamins your body craves, for they are harmless to the body. Marriage is a better alternative to an addiction to pornography, or fornication, (Zina).

The conditions of marriage in Islam are very simple, but some cultures make the act of marriage in Islam one of difficulty by standing in the way because they disagree with perhaps the culture, nationality, or the Hue (color) of the person.

> ### *Obstacles and Challenges Old Friends:*

Once you decide to embrace Islam and become a Muslim not all of your old friends will be all right with your decision. They will question you about your decision, they make it seem as though you have made such a hasty decision in their opinion to become Muslim and embrace Islam. Only because they have their preconceived ideas, about what a Muslim is like, that Muslims are not righteous, and Muslims are terrorists. Some of your old friends will attempt to call you back to the life of a Kufr (disbeliever) and the rest will stay away from you for fear that you may get into harsh debates with them and request that they become a Muslim as well.

Even though Allah (s.w.t) says in the Qur'an, you must call everyone towards Islam but not by force. There is no compulsion to become a Muslim, but you should be able to develop a healthy dialogue with your old friends and help them to understand what they view as this sudden change to the Deen of Islam. You can do this by setting an exemplary example, becoming that role model, and displaying that righteous character you learned from being a Muslim then perhaps your old friends will attend Jummah services with you to listen to the khutbah (message) of an Imam. There is no need in Islam to make your old friends an enemy they will do that of their own free will. Surah Az-Zukhruf: 43 talks of such behaviors from friends.

Qur'an Az-Zukhruf: 43 [64-67]

> [64] "Surely, it is Allah who is my Rabb and your Rabb, so worship Him. This is the Right Way." [65] "Despite these teachings, the factions disagreed among themselves, so woe to the wrongdoers from the punishment of a painful Day." [66] "Are they only waiting for the Hour of Doom—that which it should come upon them suddenly, while they are unaware?" [67] "On that day, even friends will become enemies to one another except the righteous people."

Allow them to see the light in your new Deen (way of life) faith by presenting Islam to them through your humbling peaceful actions. You never know they may decide to embrace Islam after watching your behavior and how you handle uncomfortable situations in life. You may be the one with the permission of Allah, to shed light on some unanswered questions they have about Islam.

> ➢ *Obstacles and Challenges As a Student and at Work:*

Rather you are a student in a public or private school as a Muslim there are still Obstacles and Challenges for you to face. Learning in a private Islamic school can be very challenging because of the various ideologies cultural behaviors and habits of the parents that trickle down to the children on the proper etiquette when practicing the *Five Pillars of Islam, The Articles of Faith, and Islamic laws.*

The students all wear identical attire and follow a dual curriculum comprising both Islamic studies and the standard state educational syllabus. Despite the benefits, significant obstacles arise from conflicting family values, cultural differences, nationalities, and familial traditions.

Transitioning from a private Islamic school to a public school presents unforeseen challenges for both parents and children. It becomes challenging to uphold Islamic teachings when others' beliefs do not align with your own. As a new Muslim, it's important to guide yourself and your children through the process of embracing and understanding the significance of wearing the Hijab (head covering) and Abayas (dress) for females, and the Tahj (head covering) and "Jalabiya" (traditional dress) for males.

Encouraging pride in these garments can be a gradual process, and it's essential to equip yourself with knowledge about Islam to better handle any challenges that may arise. This knowledge will not only empower you and your family but also enable you to share the beauty of Islam with others in a respectful and approachable manner. By engaging in open and meaningful conversations about faith, you can inspire understanding and compassion without coming across as overbearing. Select the educational institution that would best suit the ideology of the entire family whether it be an Islamic private school or a public non-Islamic school. Choose a school that, your children would fit in with, a school that has a large enrollment of Muslim students, if possible, you will be helpless in the public school you chose for the children because there zoned by the district. Don't become discouraged about the education your children will receive, instead make every effort to help them over the obstacles and challenges by strengthening their educational knowledge of Deen-ul Islam within the confounds of your home.

> ## *Obstacles and Challenges in the Community:*

If you were living in an Islamic community, you would think all is well and everyone gets along quite well with each other as Muslims. Asiah has experienced living in an Islamic State the Country of Qatar for eight months, with the many Masjids practically on every other four to five blocks was rather wonderful. The social functions the Country of Qatar held were refreshing and the fact that the majority of businesses had no work on Saturdays or Fridays (Jummah) which is every Muslim's Holy day rather they are practicing the Deen or not. Even though we are Muslims you still can notice the different social groups when people are out and about in the social areas but at the Masjid the social interaction was very different because it felt so much more like a family.

It was difficult only because the social skills were just not there. The cause for the difficult social mishap was the language barrier. Asiah not being able to speak the Arabic language did not stop any of the sisters and brothers from attempting to learn about who she was, and where she was from after they introduced themselves. Then Asiah began to receive invites to their homes and those who knew how to speak the English language to communicate did so willingly and cheerfully. As the sisters taught Asiah how to converse with them in Arabic while she communicated with them in English, the atmosphere was filled with delight and enjoyment.

Upon realizing how frequently Asiah visited the Masjid, the sisters dropped their initial reservations and warmly welcomed her to Qatar. They inquired about her experience in the country and how she was adjusting to life there. Asiah candidly admitted that her initial arrival in Qatar wasn't without its challenges, as she encountered significant cultural differences. Despite this, she expressed her deep appreciation for the peaceful ambiance in Qatar and the freedom to live in an Islamic state without being coerced into conforming to Islamic dress codes as a non-Muslim. She noted that people in Qatar were free to enjoy social activities with their families and friends as long as they abided by the laws of Shari'ah. Asiah also observed that Qatar placed a strong emphasis on maintaining peace and prioritized the welfare of women.

Asiah felt a deep sense of love for Allah in the country and highlighted the excellent medical facilities, particularly praising the state-of-the-art hospital that specifically catered to women. Moreover, she cherished the freedom to work with or without her face veil and full Hijab body covering. There are various types of Muslims in terms of nationality, If you reside in Qatar, you have those Masjids that speak only Arabic and then you have Masjids that translate Arabic to English, Asiah frequently visits both because she loves hearing Arabic, hearing the Arabic helps her learn it better. The sisters were kind enough to translate for her so that she could understand what the Khutbah (sermon) was about. Our festive holiday of Ramadan was truly the best for Asiah it created a bond of sisterhood that felt like no other.

Shopping at the Malls and stores was amazing all you noticed was a sea of International harmony, with men, women, and children dressed and covered up modestly. However, Asiah felt her duty as a Muslim was to extend greetings to all that she encountered even if they did not respond to her in the same manner.

Asiah's travels to Ghana West Africa, were so different from her visit to Qatar because the Muslims from Ghana did not have an issue with greetings when they noticed you walking past. In Asiah's opinion, the reason for the warm reception was that the people were all of the same hue (color) which made the approach easier than that of Qatar.

Then there is living in a community that is multi-culture Muslims, and non-Muslims. The challenge here was to enlighten those who had no idea about Deen-ul Islam. It is the duty of every Muslim to take the opportunity to show that we are a peaceful people and that what we want for ourselves is what we want for our neighbors, family, and friends, this is what Islam teaches us as Muslims, may Allah (s.w.t) make it easy for us. The Qur'an teaches us to come together on what is most common. There is no reason to prejudge an individual for the faith in which they are practicing. Get to understand who they are and what their beliefs are before you jump to any conclusions you can miss a great friend and neighbor.

(Qur'an A'l-e-'Imran: 3 [64])

> (64) "Say: "O people of the Book! Let us get together on what is common between us and you: that we shall worship none but Allah; that we shall not associate any partners with Him; that we shall not take from among ourselves any lords beside Allah." If they reject your invitation, then tell them: "Bear witness that we are Muslims (who have surrendered to Allah)."

The Qur'an acknowledges the existence of the "people of the Book," which refers to Christians and Jews who are recognized as custodians of the Book. The Tawrat (Torah) and the Injeel (Gospel) are specifically mentioned, and it is universally accepted that Prophet Ibrahim (Abraham), Isa (Jesus), Musa (Moses), and Nuh (Noah) are respected as Prophets and Messengers appointed by Allah. As a "New Muslim," it's important to recognize these shared beliefs and values to uphold the non-discriminatory principles outlined in the Qur'an.

(Qur'an Surah Ali-'Imran: 3(84)

> [84] "...We do not discriminate between any one of them and to Allah do we submit ourselves as Muslims."

One should comprehend that in Islam, the declaration "La ilaha illallah" emphasizes the belief that there is no deity worthy of worship except for Allah. This statement underscores the fundamental concept of monotheism and the exclusive devotion to Allah, rejecting the worship of any other gods or beings, including human beings.

It signifies the central tenet of the Islamic faith and the recognition of Allah as the one true God to whom Muslims should wholeheartedly submit and devote themselves

(Qur'an Al-Mumtahanah: 60: [5-6]

(5) "Our Rabb, Do not make us a victim of the unbelievers. Forgive us, our Rabb! You are the All-Mighty, the All-Wise."
(6) "Truly, in those there is an excellent example for everyone who puts his hopes in Allah and the Last Day. He that gives no heed should know that Allah is free of all wants, worthy of all praise."

To all "New Muslims" keep your prayers to Allah (s.w.t) for He is surely worthy of praise Allah is a lifeline to our salvation. Muslims should incur the praises of Allah (Ta'ala) rather than His wrath upon us as his punishment for not following the revelations of the Qur'an, the Sunnah of the Prophet (s.a.w.s) his ways according to authentic Sahih Hadiths.

[Qur'an Surah Al-Furqan 25: 69]

(69) "And his punishment shall be doubled on the Day of Resurrection and in disgrace he shall abide forever,"

Therefore, the call is to all Muslims new and seasoned to pick up your Qur'ans and read them along with the authentic Hadiths which are known as the Sunnah of (the actions, sayings, and practices of the Prophet, s.a.w.s), understand your Deen (way of life or faith) through the readings of Allah's Books it has a wealth of life's preventions and the antidote to keeping the whisper Iblis (Shaytan, c.h) away.

The Qur'an is the antidote to life's issues and the Sunnah is the path to changing our character towards an understanding knowledgeable Muslim of peace. Read the Qur'an regularly because this type of behavior will help in assisting in your studies and learning of the prescribed guidance and laws revealed to the Prophet (s.a.w.s) through the angel Gabriel by permission of Allah (s.w.t).

Remember learning is power and those who seek knowledge about all things in this life and not just Islam but on the faiths of others as well can be better informed to do their duty in the propagating of Islam. These are some of the ways that helped Asiah keep her Ibadah (faith) as she performed Salah (prayer) and continued holding on to the rope of Allah.

Even though Islam is Asiah's faith of choice she embarks on the study of other religions so that she is better informed about the faith of others which gives her the ability to communicate effectively without sounding as if she is not interested in what others think or practice in life.

Learning to understand the thought process of those who have the notion that Muslims are blind followers of Islamic beliefs, doctrine, and the Prophet. Other faith-based individuals should have a conversation with Muslims who are not looking to change or coerce them into becoming a member of the Islamic faith, but instead are attempting to learn and understand their faith and why they chose to walk that particular religious path in life. Asiah understands the way to help others accept Islam is not by insulting their faith and beliefs, but by showing others in comparison the similarities in Islam, Christianity, and Judaism this would help in building a community of various faiths on the premises of understanding the Most High, as being the one and only true creator above all religious faiths.

CHAPTER ELEVEN

CHOICE OF FRIENDS

Allah commanded us in the Qur'an. (Surah: 9 [ayah 119]

(119) "Oh, you who believe fear Allah and stay with the truthful."

The type of friends you associate with will play a significant role in your life as a Muslim. Friends who are too shy to call you for Salat and teach you properly about Islam are not the type of friends you should be spending your time with. If you have friends who are Muslims with good intentions who live some distance away from you. You should reach out to that long-distance good Muslim who will assist you in staying on the path to Allah, this is far better than any Muslim or non-Muslim that don't have your best interest at heart because Allah talks about those who profess to believe in Allah as the only deity but behind your back, they speak evil of Islam. Surrounding yourself with those friends from a long distance that will help you continue on the path of righteousness is better than being near a friend who will not keep you on that same path of righteousness. As you, study the laws of Islam recorded within the Qur'an, and the Sunnah of the Prophet Muhammad, s.a.w.s. (Ahmed, his given name by his mother), and the practice of the *Five Pillars of Islam.'* As a "New Muslim," with the constant reading of the Qur'an, you too will be known as a good Muslim with the best of intentions who would be ready to help others further their growth while guiding another Muslim on the righteous path to Islam.

Now I am going to highlight some pointers on **"Who is a good Muslim,"** according to what Allah says in the Qur'an Surah Al-Fuqan: 25, these are the good Muslims as prescribed in the Qur'an that will "surely be the ones who will be rewarded with the lofty (exalted) places in paradise for their patience, wherein they shall be welcomed with greetings and salutations."[75]

(Qur'an Surah Al-Fuqan 25: Ayah 67,69,70,72-74) says.

A good Muslim is:

- ..." One who when they spend are neither extravagant nor stingy, but keep a balance..."[67]
- ..." One who doesn't invoke any other god besides Allah, nor kill any soul which Allah has made sacred..."And One who doesn't commit fornication..."[69]
- ..." One who repents becomes a true believer, and starts doing good deeds..."[70]
- ... "One who does not bear witness to falsehood..."[72]
- ..." One who when reminded about the revelations of their Rabb, do not turn a blind eye and a deaf ear to them."[73]
- And one who prays: "Our Rabb! Make our wives and children, the comfort of our eyes and make us leaders of the righteous."[74]

The ex-husband Usman and Asiah understood that it is a far greater sacrifice, as a "New Muslim," to always surround yourself with the best of those who are striving towards the way of Allah (s.w.t) and the Sunnah of the Prophet Muhammad, s.a.w.s. (Ahmed, given name by his mother) so that you can become a stronger Muslim in the pursuit of practicing your Deen and staying on the peaceful road to success.

Now you must also understand while committing to your walk along the path of Islam to achieve your closeness with Allah (s.w.t) there will be people who will attempt to get close to you for various reasons and not all of them will come in the name of peace, for righteousness' sake or with the heart of Allah (s.w.t) nor the character of the Prophet Muhammad (Ahmed, given name by his mother).

Many may not even have true knowledge of Islam because they are pretenders Kufr (unbelievers) they may and will deal with you harshly just to make augmentation from you because they feel as though they have been practicing Islam longer, so they know better than you do as a "New Muslim." For instance, the Qur'an says,

Qur'an Surah A'l-e-'Imran: 3: [118])

(118) "O believers! Do not make intimate friendships with any but your people. The unbelievers will not miss any opportunity to corrupt you. They desire nothing but your destruction: their malice has become evident from what they say, and what they conceal in their hearts is far worse. We have made our revelations plain to you if you want to understand."

There are those individuals who will attempt to discourage you from your practice by their attitudes about Islam, those people who often hold on to the extremist point of view and misinform you about what is *"Harm"* and what is *"Halal"* and then tell you of books that were written by those who make claims that these are the words of the Prophet (s.a.w.s) when they are not. When you find yourself in these types of situations, just go to the Surahs within the Qur'an read them, and the <u>Sahih Hadiths by Bukhari and Muslims</u> then research for yourself the information. To achieve a clear understanding of it seek out an Imam for clarification but you must also understand that as a Muslim you have the right to question any information that seems to be suspect and if there happens to be any discrepancy between the Qur'an and the Hadiths you must follow what the Qur'an is saying.

Qur'an al-Anbiya: 21: [73] says.

> (73) "We gave him a son Ishaq (Isaac) and then a grandson Yaqoob (Jacob), and we made each of them a righteous man." (72) We made them leaders who guided other people by our command, and we sent them revelations to do good deeds, establish Salah (prayers), and pay Zakah (obligatory charity). Us alone did they serve."

What this ayah is saying is that Allah (s.w.t) made them Imams who guided people by 'His' command and revealed to them about doing good deeds and establishing Salah (prayer) and Zakah (charity) and to Allah (s.w.t) alone they would serve nothing or anyone else. This is why each of the Masjids we visit always has an Imam in service of the Muslim Ummah (Community) when there is a need for advice, marriage ceremony, and other activities.

Islam is not always about **Haram! Haram! Haram!** Asiah's ex-husband Usman said he uses a simple yardstick when choosing his friends which is to observe and listen to what they are talking about, people who always base everything they do according to Allah's Commandments, the Qur'an, and the Sunnah of Islam, are the ones he socializes with. As for Asiah the people who love to stay within the limits of Islam, the ones who guide you with truth and challenge you to research the information for yourself and not just take their word for it, are someone who has a greater fear of Allah then trying to make cool points with her.

More times than not you will know a person by the way they approach you and you can feel the spirit and character that is living within them.

Their sincere faith and commitment to Islam would be evident in their behavior and demeanor, where you could see the illumination (insight) of Allah (s.w.t.) within them. So, surround yourself with those who have true Taqwwa (piety, consciousness of Allah) and those who protect themselves from the evil deeds of mankind. One should be afraid of Allah when they have followed the whispering deceptions of Shaitan (the cursed one). Those who go against all of the good guidance that Allah has decreed for all Muslims and mankind to obey the Laws and revelations of the Qur'an and follow the Sunnah (traditions and character) of His Prophet Muhammad, s.a.w.s.(Ahmed, his given name by his mother). Any Muslim who has the true spiritual character of goodness, most times is revealed to you when they speak and by their actions.

These Muslims are strong enough in their Iman (faith) to help strengthen your Islamic character to make you a better Muslim; they are the ones who are leading by a good Islamic model behavior when you see them, they are happy about being a Muslim and not embarrassed by Islam. This type of behavior will move people to approach you and ask questions about your Deen (way of life or faith). Also, remember that the Qur'an speaks about those who pretend to love you, care for you, and respect Islam but behind your back, they are saying other things. Islam informs you about such individual persons so be aware and listen carefully; pay close attention to what others are saying about Islam and the way you should be practicing it.

The Qur'an ('Al-e-'Imran: 3 [119]) says.

---

[119] "Whereas you love them, they do not love you even though you believe in their Holy Books the Psalms, the Torah, and the Gospels). When they meet you, they say, "We also

> believe in your prophet and you're Qur'an;" but when they are alone, they bite their fingertips in rage against you. Say to them: "May you perish in your rage;" surely Allah knows all the secrets of the heart."

Islam has always been a blessing of peace for Asiah in whatever condition she found herself in here on this earth. Of course, when things were going negatively in this life as a human being, Asiah questioned the reasons why this was happening to her so often. Most times she had come to realize that when things happen that we are dissatisfied with, we become angry with Allah, the Most High (God) for allowing it to happen. However, most times these obstacles placed before us are for our good, and for the benefit of receiving something far greater than what we have lost, and most times we walk right into harm's way knowing the chance we take or the choice we have willingly made, may not be the right one. At this instance, Asiah is speaking in terms of materialistic values more so than human loss of life, even then, loss of life can be a blessing when a person has been suffering for quite a long period. When things seem to be so very difficult for Asiah, she often go into a state of isolation turn to Allah (s.w.t), performing not just obligatory prayer but voluntary prayers as well with such sincerity of heart, asking If she have offended 'Him' in any way that 'He' forgive her for any sins she has committed against Him, and please accept her Salah (prayers) of repentance, by showering her with 'His Compassion, 'His Mercy and 'His Forgiveness.

Allow me to ask this question; have you been blessed with good fortune by the will of Allah, the Most High (God) that others would hate you or even dislike you for no reason? There is also a Surah in the Qur'an that warns you against such people and how to protect yourself from them.

The Qur'an ('Al-e-'Imran: 3 [120]) says.

[120] "When you are blessed with good fortune, they grieve; but if some misfortune overtakes you, they rejoice. If you are patient and guard yourselves against evil, their schemes will not harm you in any way. Surely, Allah encompasses all their actions."

This is a personal story; the year was 2012. The first time Asiah was allowed to travel to the Continent of Ghana West Africa. Once she reached the airport of RDU (Raleigh Durham International) her documents passed through immigration and she boarded the airplane on her way to London Heathrow Airport, the flight went great it landed safely.

There was a six-hour layover before her next flight to Ghana West Africa but when she reached immigration for her next flight Asiah was detained because there was no Ghana Visa inside of her passport. Shaitan(c.h.)was working to bring her back to America but she was determined to reach my destination. Once it had been disclosed that the Ghana immigration Office said she just needed to have 150 Ghana cedi when she landed in Accra to receive a Visa on arrival, which Asiah had. However, London immigration was not going to allow her to board the flight until a Visa had been obtained. The airline put her up in a hotel for one night with a food allowance and for the next two days, she lived in the airport until her scheduled appointment to meet with the Ghana High Commission of London to get the Visa on Monday morning. Before the appointment, she stayed inside of the airports Masjid making Du'aa prayers to Allah asking that he please forgive her of any sins and accept her prayers, filled with tears while her heart was just pouring with grief.

Asiah found herself out of money because now there was this need to use her extra money to purchase a Visa in London. Asiah said that Allah (s.w.t) worked his miracles for her yes, indeed He did. Others noticed her in the airport for two days and began to inquire as to the reason for her being in the airport. Even the airport police approached her. Once she told her story Allah (s.w.t) sent her these six angels to assist in her journey, (an angel of protection, two angels with money, one angel of help who was a captain, for Virgin Airlines and Muslim, and one with guidance on how to travel the trains and buses in London).

After her appointment, she was given a Visa for Ghana, but she missed her flight due to the airline not allowing her to board without the visa, even though Ghana has visa on arrival. The airline scheduled Asiah for another flight to Ghana West Africa one without having to pay, and she was finally on her way to Ghana, Africa. This is just one of the many reasons why no one can tell Asiah that Allah (s.w.t) doesn't have a hand in her life so long as she continues to walk her righteous path of faith by following the revelations of the Qur'an and the Sunnah of His Prophet (s.a.w.s). Therefore no one could shake her Iman (faith) no matter what circumstance she face in this life. So just hold on tight to the rope of Allah (s.w.t), the Qur'an, and the Sunnah of the Prophet Muhammad (s.a.w.s), and all shall be well with you (Insha Allah) meaning if Allah, wills. There is also an 'ayah' in the Qur'an that speaks of holding on to the rope of Allah it is as follows in part:

The Qur'an (Surah Ali 'Imran: 3[103]) says.

(103) "And all together hold fast to the rope of Allah (Faith of Islam) and be not divided among yourselves...."

When Allah (s.w.t) instructed the family of Ali 'Imran, as a people, <u>not to become divided</u>. People from all nationalities that embraced Islam were once enemies. Until they accepted Islam and took their Shahadah, declaring (La illaha ill Allah). Islam is so very international in many ways; in language, culture, and family traditions yet when we as Muslims enter any of the Masjids around the world, we all stand shoulder to shoulder, prostrating before Allah in Unisom reciting the same Arabic language. What other Deen (way of life or faith) do you know of that does this besides Islam?

The Qur'an Surah A'l-e-'Imran: 3 [105]) further says.

---

[105] "Be not like those, who became divided into sects and who started to argue against each other after clear revelations had come to them. Those responsible for division and arguments will be sternly punished."

While keeping those who mean you no good away through prayer and selecting a good choice of friends to surround yourself with like Muslims who have the best of intentions in their deeds and their hearts.

Remember Surah A'l-e-'Imran [103] instructing you to hold on to the rope of Allah meaning hold on to your new faith of Islam, the words of Allah within the Qur'an and the Sunnah (traditions of) 'His, Prophet (s.a.w.s). When the going gets rough get into your position of Salah (prayer) and praise Allah as Musa (Moses) prayed:

(Ta-Ha: 20: [25-28])

---

[25] "O my Rabb! Open my heart, ease my task [26] and remove the impediment from my speech [27] so that people may understand what I say."[28]

Allah is the grantor of Mercy (Ar-Raheem) and the giver of this life. When we begin to propagate Islam as instructed by Allah we pray as Musa (Moses) prayed that He, too make our task and remove any type of speech impediment so that when we talk and others listen, they can understand what we are saying about Islam as being a faith of peace instead of a faith of war.

According to Qur'an Al- 'Anam: 6: [116]:

> "If you were to obey the majority of those who live on earth, they will lead you away from Allah's path. They only follow idle fancies, indulging in conjecture."

Also, according to Qur'an Surah 3 ayah 7: The Holy Qur'an came along with the practices of prayers and worshiping Allah.

Qur'an Ali 'Imran: 3: [7]

> "It is He who has sent down to you, the Book; in it are verses (that are) precise – they are the foundation of the Book – and others unspecific. As for those whose hearts is deviation (from truth), they will follow that of it which is unspecific, seeking discord and seeking an interpretation (suitable to them). And no one knows it's (true) interpretation except Allah. But those firm in knowledge say, "We believe in it. All (of it) is from our Lord." And no one will be reminded except those of understanding."

Therefore, choose your friends wisely and guard yourselves from those who wish to take you away from your path of righteousness. Better association is the key to a successful life.

CHAPTER TWELVE

MAINTAINING A MODERATE PRACTICE

(Qur'an al-Baqarah: 2: [143])

(143) "We have made you a moderate Ummah (nation) so that you may testify against mankind and that your own Rasool may testify against you. We decreed your former Qiblah only to distinguish those who are the real followers of the Rasool from those who would turn away from the faith. It was indeed a hard test except for those whom Allah has guided. Allah does not want to make your faith fruitless. Allah is Compassionate and Merciful to mankind."

This ayah does not mean Muslims should abandon the practice of the *Five Pillars of Islam* nor should we abandon any other laws of Fiqh (Islamic Jurisprudence) such as our dress code and partaking of 'Haram' activities doing these things will place you in the den of 'Sinful' acts of behaviors.

No Muslim is allowed to alter the prescribed Islamic practices according to their convenience. This ayah is simply stating that Allah has now changed the direction of Salah (prayers), in that we may know who the true followers of Deen-ul Islam are, and the Sunnah (Traditions) of His Prophet (s.a.w.s). Allah (s.w.t) has encouraged us as Muslims to be moderate in all things not only in acts of worship but also in our daily activities. Too much excess of anything can burn one out. Let us talk about the Five Pillars of Islam; now as Muslims, we are required to make Salah (prayers), to give Zakah (charity), to 'Fast' for (Ramadan), and to make Haj (pilgrimage) if and when we are financially able.

When we talk of maintaining moderate practice in Islam, we are talking about not overexerting one's body by the performance of too many salat (prayer). When your body tells you that it is tired, please listen, and stop what you are doing. Even though we are required to give to charity by helping the needy and the poor it so not require that, we exhaust all of our financial means to do so leaving our families with nothing to live on. Then there is the obligatory fasting for Ramadan, which is for thirty days within a month Allah is not asking that we starve ourselves or our family, it just requires that we fast during Salaatul Fajr until Salaatul Maghrib during the month of Ramadan. When the sun sets (end) is when we break our fast. The Islamic Haj (pilgrimage) is required according to one's financial means and at least once before one dies. Those Muslims who are wealthy enough to travel for Hajj should not do so in excess after all Allah (s.w.t) on the Day of Judgment will look at the intentions of your heart and not how many times you made Hajj. Help other poor Muslims make the journey of Hajj allowing them to complete the fifth pillar of Islam.

This is what we mean by maintaining moderate practice as a Muslim to ensure normality in our lives, and the avoidance of behaving excessively or extremely other than what has been ordained for our lives as Muslims. New Muslims often tend to learn Islam fast and in doing so they attempt to perform so much of Ibadah (worship) to surpass other Muslims. Then after a while the spirit starts going down and the practice becomes less.

First, we need to understand that paradise is not about how much you do but how much you did well and were accepted by Allah (s.w.t).

The Prophet (s.a.w.s) said.

"The best type of worship is the one that is little and constant."

When you find you have accomplished your mission and have done enough to see Allah's pleasure, just be mindful of how He (Allah) has demonstrated to the Prophet (s.a.w.s) through the angel (Gabriel) the proper ways in which to practice Islam. The key to moderate practice is sound Islamic knowledge, which is essential for all Muslims. Emotion makes a "New Muslim" woman want to put on a Niqab (Veil face covering) but find opposition from the masses of the people after a while they remove their Niqab. A wise man once said; "when you give up you will stay up but when you jump up you will fall." Within the Bible Proverbs 24: 16 it says, "For a righteous man may fall seven times and rise again, but the wicked shall fall by calamity." Maintaining moderation is to be consistent in all that you do and ensure you do it the correct way. When we talk about moderation it means not to go to the extremes of the five pillars of Islam and the extremes of the articles of faith. Example: Asiah's ex-husband Usman and herself are cut from two very different clothes in the Deen (way of life or faith) of Islam.

What Asiah is attempting to tell you is that her ex-husband Usman, who is from Nigeria Africa is always giving her different proverbs of what the elders in his country would often say. Their cultural background and dialogue of language are very different including the English language.

Usman speaks several languages fluently while Asiah speak one language fluently and parts, bits, and pieces of other languages. The funny thing is that he does not get these proverbs mixed up with how he practices his Deen (way of life or faith). He is always at the Masjid (Mosque) praying, and sometimes he even falls asleep in the Masjid until the next prayer time. He makes it his business to hurry for Jummah (Friday congregational prayer) at times leaving Asiah behind because she always need to look so perfect when praising Allah.

Now what Asiah started doing was getting up earlier for Jummah so that she could beat him to the Masjid. It is funny now that she is reflecting on it; the best thing about it is he's always coaching her with Ibadah (worship) as she does him. They are a team in Islam whenever they both fall short, they strengthen each other by encouraging one another to follow through.

While Usman is great with keeping his prayers on time, Asiah great with reading and studying the Qur'an and other doctrines because she loves to read. Not that he does not like to read, it is just from the time he learned about his family's weakness in Islam they had him in many Quranic classes and he has memorized at least 40% of the Qur'an in his heart in Arabic. He is from the family tribe 'Yoruba' they are very religious people, kind so far as Asiah have experienced.

The reason Asiah is telling this story is to help you understand that surrounding yourself with Muslims who have the best intentions can cause your journey through Islam to be beautiful. Sometimes on different occasions Usman and Asiah would create a plan of commitment to perform more Salah (prayers) than is required especially when there is trouble or when we wish to ask something extra of Allah and to show him how much we appreciate his Mercy upon our family. We both have had our times of obstacles and challenges in this life.

We receive all types of whispers from Shaytan (c.h) attempting to sway us from Allah and his Mercy but we both pray, and sure enough, Allah makes it happen. This is what Iman (faith) is all about, there is nothing like it. Sure, doubt will creep in but the both of us dawn our badges of encouragement to one another, we teach one another different things we have learned in our travels, and Deen (way of life or faith) we do our very leveled best to keep our vibes positive keeping the negative at a very low state. When it comes, we pray, release it to Allah Ta'ala and so shall it be.

We keep ourselves grounded in Islam so as not to become, an extremist with our Deen (way of Life or faith) that is why we love it so much we can maintain our righteous walk to Allah with moderate practices. Usman has taught Asiah a great deal about being humble. This walk towards the Deen of Islam is a lifelong journey, and being humble, tolerant, and respectful of the faiths of others while maintaining your Ibadah (faith) in Islam is a practice every Muslim should desire in their journey towards Islam.

CHAPTER THIRTEEN

PREPARING FOR DEATH

The Qur'an (Surah Ali 'Imran: 3: [185]) states.

(185) "Every soul shall taste death, and you will only be given your [full] compensation on the Day of Resurrection. So, he who is drawn away from the Fire and admitted to Paradise has attained [his desire]. And what is the life of this world except the enjoyment of delusion."

Death is irreversible and it is not something humanity would always like to talk about in the open. Death is not determined by age or achievement in life but by the time decreed for us by Allah (s.w.t). The Prophet (s.a.w.s) said; "Prepare for death as if you will not witness tomorrow." Constantly remember that death can come to you at any moment and the angel of death does not need to notify you of 'His coming. Death will not wait for you to get married nor will death wait for you to follow the ways of Allah (s.w.t) and the Sunnah of His Prophet Muhammad, s.a.w.s. (Ahmed, his given name by his mother). Remember that death has no respect for age or time therefore you should strive in your Deen (way of life or faith) to do good deeds always and Allah will forgive your sins. How would you like your last moments on Earth to be? Surely not that of a morally bankrupt soul! Surely not that of someone who died and did not bother to make good his debt to those whom he owed; this is the reason Allah (s.w.t) has instructed all Muslims to prepare for death by making out a last "Will" so that your family will not need to fight over what you have left on this earth. Your family shouldn't have to struggle to find ways to source money to bury your remains.

A practical way of remembering death is to make a self-evaluation at night before resting. Consider going to bed and never awakening, have you settled all of your debts, have you arranged your burial, are your finances sorted out, so that your family can pay people what you owe them, and they can retrieve what is owed to you? Write all of these financial transactions out to make it easy on your family upon your death. According to a Hadith, "If a debtor died when he still owed money to people, they will take from his Hasanaat (good deeds) whatever is in accordance with what he owes them."

In Sunnah ibn Majah, narrated with Sahih Isnad that Ibn Umar (May Allah be pleased with him), Stated in; Sahih Al-Jaami

[Sahih Al-Jaami As-Sagheer, 5/537, Hadith No. 6432)

"The Messenger of Allah (s.a.w.s.) said; "Whoever dies owing a Dinar or a Dirham it will be paid from his Hasanaat (good deeds), for then there will be no Dinars or Dirhams."

It is said in the Qur'an. (Surah Al-Anbiya: 21: [47]

---

[47] "On the Day of Judgement, we shall set up scales of justice so that no one will be dealt with unjustly in any way; even if someone has an act as small as a grain of mustard seed, we will bring it to account, and sufficient are we to settle the accounts."

Also, the Qur'an talks about the payment of debts in terms of the distribution of inheritance.

(Surah Al-Nisa: 4: [12]

---

(12) "You shall inherit one half of your wives' estate if they leave no child, but if they leave behind a child then you will get one-fourth of their estate, after fulfilling the terms of their last will and the payment of debts. Your wives shall inherit one-fourth if you leave no child behind you; but if you leave a child, then they shall get one-eighth of your estate; after fulfilling the terms of your last will and the payment of debts…This is the commandment of Allah. Allah is knowledgeable, forbearing."

Remember that other people's property or money if not returned in this world you shall have to return it on the Day of Judgment with the good deeds you have done while you were alive. If what you are to return is more than your *'Good Deeds'* (Hasanaat) then the *'Bad or Evil Deeds'* (Saiyyat) of the owners equal to what is owed, will be added to your account. Make plans to settle all your debts. Many people are not so worried about the debts owed to them. Others may have forgotten about the debt, even still you the debtor and the lender will both be shown on the Day of Judgment from the records of the angels that are keeping account of each person's deeds on earth, both good and bad deeds. Being a good conscious, Muslim of everything you do in this life for your two angels are recording it all for use against you to determine whether Allah (s.w.t) will admit you into Paradise or Hell Fire. According to the Islamic law of inheritance in the Qur'an states.

(Surah Al-Baqarah: 2: [180]

> (180) "The 'Will' is made obligatory before the death of anyone of you who is leaving some property behind, to bequeath it equitably to his parents and relatives. This is a duty incumbent on the righteous."

A Muslim should draw up a sound "Will" not just for his family members but to keep other authorities from taking what is rightly the inheritance of the family members. So, before we are called to move away from this worldly life, please complete your 'Will' a document that will provide your family with peace of mind. Helping them to understand your debts so they may use your money if there is any to pay off people you owe money to. Help your family in the division of any property that you may have left behind and finally leave them instructions and an insurance policy for your final burial rights. All those who don't wish to follow the instruction of the deceased and you wish to contest the Last 'Testament this is fine but understand that you will bring confusion within the family. The sole purpose of leaving a will is so the family won't see the need to argue over the left property of their beloved deceased family member. Allah (Ta'ala) will be the final judge in Janna (the afterlife).

(Qur'an A'l-e'Imran: 3[102])

> Remember that Allah (s.w.t) said (102) "...do not die accept in the position of submission."

Therefore, ensure that you have insurance for your final burial arrangements to help relieve your family members of the burden of having to foot the bill. We must lighten the burdens because the grief of the passing of a loved one can be difficult to get through. Yet, still it would be in our best interest to ensure the loved ones we leave behind do not have to fight over property or solicit money from anyone for your final burial.

CHAPTER FOURTEEN

THE RIGHTEOUS WALK TO ALLAH

[Qur'an Surah Al-Furqan 25: 63]

(63) "True servants of the Compassionate (Allah) are those who walk on the earth in humility and when the ignorant people address them, they say: "Peace;"(63)

Simple good behavior is enough of an impact and a reference for others in this society and Muslims alike. As a Muslim, you hold the responsibility to sharpen your behaviors as that of the reported life of the Prophet (s.a.w.s) character. Live a life of modest humbling means that would exemplify you in the sight of Allah (s.w.t). Each day Asiah says, she is blessed to be awoken by the breath of Allah (s.w.t) Asiah states, she is eternally grateful for such a blessing in life. As she prepare for the early morning "Fajr" (prayer) as the call of adhan is ringing in her ears as she struggle to get out of that bed of comfort. In all honesty, sometimes she do not make it out of the bed for "Fajr" prayer. She begin to pray lying down where she ask for the forgiveness of Allah for not running to the call of the adhan. However, the times that she was able to make that call to prayer were the best times of her life because prayer cleanses the soul in ways only an individual experience can understand. Meeting the "Fajr" prayer is the greatest prayer of them all in Asiah's opinion.

Fajr prayer gives you a sense of renewing your faith in Allah (s.w.t) while allowing you to have a brighter brand-new day to actualize your dreams. The righteous walk to Allah is not an easy journey with the many temptations we face in this Dunya (world) every single day. The many obstacles and challenges we face like; the loss of employment, a home, not having enough food for yourself and the children if your married or not, and the sad disappointing look on your child's face, when you are unable to help them get by in life financially, but they can look out for you as a parent. This is what Allah (s.w.t) revealed to the Prophet (s.a.w.s) many ayahs talk about the care of parents here is one.

(Qur'an Surah An-Nisa 4: 36)

[36] "Serve Allah, and join not any partners with Him, and do good – to parents…"

Yet, you manage to maintain your righteous walk to Allah by abiding by the Pillars of Islam and preaching the doctrine of Islam to your children, their friends, and others about the peace and love you find in Islam even though life is rough. You do all of this with your daily five prayers and the prayer of Tahjud (midnight prayer), this is when you realize that you are a servant of the Compassionate (Allah) because you are praying as is instructed within the Qur'an, prostrating throughout the night. This is how Muslims should devote themselves to the righteous walk to Allah, as His servant, worshiping only Him throughout the night.

Within Qur'an Surah Al-Fuqan 25: 64] says.

(64) "…Who pass the night prostrating before their Rabb and standing in prayers…;"

If you have been shrouded with the blessings of Allah, you should know there are so many things you can do for Islam and the rewards will always be deposited into your account so long as others are benefitting from your charitable deeds and intentions. Not only those Muslims by Chance (born in Islam) can become 'Scholars' but Muslims by Choice who (accept Islam) can become 'Scholars' as well. Fight for the knowledge of your Deen (faith way of life) and never underestimate your learning capabilities. The righteous walk to Allah is not easy it is just a matter of effort and perseverance, and you too can become a light for the Ummah (Muslim Community). Think more of what you want Islam to benefit from you and not what you want to benefit from Islam, after all Allah, Created Mankind, and Jinn to worship him. Make use of all that Allah has blessed you with to propagate the Deen (faith way of life) Islam. If you are financially wealthy, you can invest in projects that will benefit the Muslim and the Islamic Ummah (Community) without the expectation of receiving any financial profit which is not 'Haraam' but the best profit is from Allah by being admitted into 'Paradise which will be the best of profits to accept.' In Surah Al-Furqan Allah revealed to the Prophet (s.a.w.s) about spending and stinginess.

[Qur'an Surah Al-Furqan 25: 67]

(67) "…Who when they spend, are neither extravagant nor stingy, but keep the balance between those two extremes…"

If you are a blessed writer, then you can write newspaper articles about Islam and volunteer your services to Islamic Media. Sectors of Islam are still lacking in the ownership of Media, and Muslims are still relying on other mediums of news to tell our stories and give our point of view about acts of terror in Islam. Muslims who are truly **following the righteous walk to** Allah have an opinion and a voice about what is happening in the world around us so they can stop painting Islam as this 'black faith' of hate instead of peace. With the news being, propagated by non-Muslims who were misinformed about the life of a truly righteous Muslim or Muslimah.

Whatever your field of study is you can always organize free tutorials for Muslim students to make them excel in their academics. This is an act of intentional good deeds, not only that you will also make an impact in the lives of children and family members alike and this is a deed that Allah will not forget nor will others when you are dead and gone from earth. If all Muslims think about how they can benefit Islam instead of what can Islam do for them Allah will guide them into Paradise and forgive any of their sins for these intentional acts of 'Good Deeds.' We can develop a stronger Islamic Ummah (Community) to achieve the independence and respect we pray for as an Islamic Ummah (Community) from others who have a misunderstanding about the true life of a believing Muslim.

(Qur'an A'l-e-'Imran: 3 [102}

Allah said "Oh you who believe! Fear Allah as He should be feared and die not except as a Muslim." [102] "…Thus, Allah makes clear his revelations to you so that you may be rightly guided."[102]

Just remember that all Muslims are required to succumb to "The Righteous Walk to Allah" as the above Surah states to fear Allah, which is having 'Taqwa' in the Deen (Religious way of life) of Islam. It also states that when we die it should be that of a

Muslim and nothing else. There are plenty of Muslims who have a weak Ibadah (worship), and a weak Iman (belief or faith), and the environment we may find ourselves living in may not be the best for our Iman (faith) it very well may pull us away from the righteous path that Allah is keeping us on. Then again, Allah allowed Shaytan (c.h) to have respite so that he may tempt us into going astray. When this happens, one can always repent to Allah, continue with our good deeds, and walk away from the bad deeds of our environment that the whisper Shaytan (c.h) will always cause us to feel as if we need it and that it is great for us. Through prayer, all things are possible so long as the intention of your heart is good, and your deeds are as well. Maintain your spirit of a true Muslim who believes in *The Articles of Faith* and the one who practices the *Five Pillars of Islam.*' After all, Allah is the one who forgives our bad deeds so long as we repent in sincerity of heart in worshiping Him. Allah (s.w.t) revealed in

Qur'an Surah 25: 70 saying.

---

(70) "…Except the one who repents, becomes a true believer, and starts doing good deeds, for then Allah will change his evil deeds into good, and Allah is Most Forgiving, Most Merciful…"
(70) [Qur'an 25: 70]

So, come on new and seasoned Muslims how about we strive in the way of Allah (s.w.t) to get our Ibadah (worship) up? Grab hold of our Imam (faith) and walk this righteous path of love, peace, and harmony to Allah (s.w.t). By committing ourselves to do those good deeds and asking Him (Allah) to ward off all of the bad whisperings of Iblis (Shaytan, c.h).

Show the world your model character like that of the Prophet (s.a.w.s) so that we may be allowed to enjoy the great ones before us in Paradise. My Muslim sisters and brothers in Islam let us learn to live together in peace and harmony despite our different Religious faiths because Allah surely refers to getting to know one another in the Qur'an.

Surah Al-Hujurat 49: 13 and it state's

> (13) "Oh humankind! We created you from a single pair of a male and a female, and made you into nations and tribes, so that you may know each other (not that you may despise each other). Verily the most honored among you in the sight of Allah is the most righteous of you. And Allah has full knowledge and is well acquainted (with all things)"

Alhamdulillah! (All praise is due to Allah) Amin! This is what we say as Muslims whether we are going through hardship or experiencing a life of eases those words are utter in praising Allah, because life comes in good and bad phases, from family, friends, employers, coworkers, children etc. Always remember to keep yourself in the company of people with positive energy because they will always keep you lifted in your spirit. Allah knows better than anyone else what is best for you so keep yourself prayerful when every you make important decisions

CHAPTER FIFTEEN

SUMMARY

FREQUENTLY ASKED QUESTIONS

1. <u>Polygamy:</u> Permitted in Islam according to the Qur'an and Sunnah, yes. But it is not an obligation.

2. <u>Hijab:</u> Required Head and body (breast) covering not the face.

3. <u>Khemaar/Niqab</u> (Veil): Face covering for women is not (obligatory) it is by choice according to the Qur'an which says there is no compulsion in Islam.

4. <u>Alcohol (Haram):</u> Forbidden or Prohibited in Islam according to the Qur'an and Sunnah the advice we abstain from intoxicants.

5. <u>Pork (Haram):</u> Forbidden or Prohibited in Islam according to the Qur'an and Sunnah.

6. <u>Life after Death (Janna):</u> Paradise for believers and Punishment (Hellfire) for the unbelievers, this is Judgement hour for all.

7. <u>Different Islamic Sects:</u> There is only but one Islam (Al-Deen-ul Fitrah); the faith of rituals but a complete way of life including (spiritual, social, economic, and

political, etc.), In addition, there is only One Creator (Jinn and Mankind). Of which Allah (s.w.t) created to worship Him alone.
8. <u>Kafir (Unbelievers)</u>: One who rejects the truth even when it is put before them with clear proof.

When Allah first decided to grace Asiah with 'His' compassion and 'His' mercy by calling her to embrace Islam. Asiah did not know how to accept this calling. Only because she was born into this world of Christianity and did not understand how she could inform her parents without offending them. Therefore, Asiah's next step, with the Bible in hand she would pray to the Most High, asking that "He please show her in the Bible how to explain the reason for her to no longer choose to eat foods that were *Haram'* (Prohibited or forbidden). Because she had learned that the eating of Swine (Pork) in Islam and Christianity is forbidden, so here she was at the kitchen table praying for guidance, and low and behold the Most High, (Allah, s.w.t) directed her to open that Bible to the Book of Leviticus, chapter 11 verse 7; and this is what she read.

Leviticus Chapter 11:7

> "And the pig, though it has a split hoof completely divided, does not chew the cud; it is unclean for you."(Chapter 11: 7)

This information from the Tawrat (Torah) and the Qur'an gave her the much-needed courage to approach her parents about why the consumption of unclean foods is no longer acceptable to her. Right away Asiah's mother stated, "You have been eating Pork all this time and you have not died yet. Then she pulled out the good old-fashioned Bible that Allah sent to the people of the Book (Tawrat) Jews and Christians through the

Prophet Musa (Moses; pbuh) and showed her the passage to read. Since that time, she has been the driving force to help Asiah fulfill her calling from Allah to accept Islam as her new, Deen (way of life or faith). As Asiah began to read the Qur'an, she also came across several Surahs' and Ayahs that refers to foods that are *'Haraam'* (forbidden or not allowed) and foods that are *'Halaal'* (permissible or allowed). The other two sources of information are from

Al-Baqarah: 2 [173]; it reads.

"He has forbidden you to eat dead, meat, blood, the flesh of swine, and that on which any name other than Allah has been invoked… (p. 136)

The other source of information is from

Al-Ma'idah: 5 [3]; it also reads.

"You are forbidden to eat the meat of any animal that dies by itself, (dead body), blood, the flesh of swine (pig meat) and that on which any name other than Allah's has been invoked…
(p.214)

Now, let us move on to the prohibition of the substance known as alcohol. In Islam, this substance known as alcohol that will cause intoxication is not allowed for any Muslim whether they are a practicing Muslim or not, Allah (s.w.t) asks that we as Muslims abstain from drinking intoxicants which is written in the Qur'an. Again, Asiah came across this information in the same two *Surahs*.

Al-Baqarah: 2 [219]; it reads,

> "They ask you about drinking and gambling. Tell them there is great sin in both, although they may have some benefit for men; but their sin is greater than their benefit." (pg. 143-4)

Then Allah follows up by reaffirming that Muslims shall not partake in the drinking of intoxicants in

Surah Al-Ma'idah: 5: [90]; and it reads,

> "O believers! Intoxicants and gambling (games of chance), dedication to stones (paying tribute to idols), and using arrows (for seeking luck or decision) are the filthy works of Shaitan. Get away from them so that you may prosper." (pg. 227-8)

Therefore, do not eat or drink that which Allah (s.w.t) has disallowed, it causes you to lose your peace. The authority and owner of peace is embedded in one of the illustrious names of Allah, (s.w.t) and that is (As-Salam) translated as "The Peace" thus saying that Allah is the creator and the authority of peace He alone has ownership of this feeling known as peace.

Therefore, Allah's instructions prohibiting the consumption of unclean foods and asking that we abstain from intoxicating drinks that can cause mood alteration as it distracts you from the remembrance of Allah (s.w.t), and the Sunnah of the Prophet,(.s.a.w.s). This is the truth of Allah, (s.w.t) has given to the Prophet Muhammad (s.a.w.s), to give to all of Mankind accept it or reject it the choice is of your own.

In the Qur'an Surah Al-Kahf: (18) Allah instructed the Prophet, (s.a.w.s) to recite.

"What has been revealed to you from the Book of your Rabb: no one is authorized to change His Words and if you dare, you will find no refuge to protect you from Him." (pg. 27)

Remember when you speak of the words of Allah (s.w.t) or rewrite them somewhere else be sure not to change any of His words. However, you can paraphrase what you have read in the Qur'an from what you have remembered reading. Now allow me to speak to the views of polygamy, most times we hear about this act of polygamy through media or word of mouth from others who are practicing this form of conscious behavior. Some agree with the arrangement and others disagree. In Islam polygamy is not at all a compulsory requirement but a choice which Allah (s.w.t), has given to Mankind who are practicing Muslims. You have some women in all truth who are being forced into such an environment and then you have those who are welcoming to the idea of it for their reasons.

However, as Asiah has previously stated polygamy is not compulsory in Islam so no one can force you to accept such behavior. Now, through her readings and her studies, she has learned there are two types of polygamy the first being "a man marries more than one woman" and the second is polyandry, "where a woman marries more than one man." Now, in Islam, polygamy is limited to only four and is permitted but polyandry is completely prohibited women are not allowed in Islam to marry more than one husband at the same time. In the Qur'an Surah An-Nisa: 4[3] Allah's instructions about polygamy are as follows.

Quran Surah (An-Nisa, pg.186)

"If you fear that you shall not be able to treat the orphans with fairness, then marry other women of your choice; two, three, or four. But if you fear that you will not be able to maintain justice between your wives, then marry only one or any slave girl you may own. That will be more suitable, so that you may not deviate from the Right Way."

So as a new Muslim when people begin to kick back about accepting or rejecting a polygamous marriage the choice at the end of the day is still of your own. Some Muslim men hide the fact that they have a first wife for several reasons, two of them that Asiah know of from experience are "fear that the woman will not accept such an arrangement and the other reason is they are looking to find greener pastures in other countries" so they opt not to mention the first wife. You see some Countries that are not of a totally Islamic State, have marriages that are not, documented through the Court, this makes it appear that the Muslim man is still a bachelor. In Asiah's opinion, polygamy can be a wonderful relationship between the co-wives if there is maturity involved and the husband treats each wife with equal standing to ensure that neither wife has seniority over the other no matter who he married first, second, third, or fourth.

Some Muslim men are just too immature or unable to deal with the demands and emotions of their wives. Then the polygamous Muslim man makes the wrong decisions in an attempt to bring his wives together in peace and harmony most times the man is the problem that hinders his wives from developing a relationship with the lies he tells to one to obtain peace and order between his wives.

Most would say that it is difficult to maintain equality in a polygamous marriage relationship. Because some sisters may have children and others may not, the funding would be different in terms of upkeep. The level of love may also be different because one wife may do something better than the other, however, the husband should never allow this to interfere with his level of respect for them and his being equitable to his wives all. For Allah (s.w.t) has revealed in the Qur'an a Surah saying.

(Aayah No. 129, Surah An-Nisa' Qur'an)

> "You will never be able to do perfect justice between wives even if it is your ardent desire, so do not incline too much to one of them to leave the other hanging. And if you do justice, and do all that is right and fear Allah, by keeping away from all that is wrong, then Allah is Ever Oft-forgiving, Most Merciful."[129]

Thus, as you can see from the Aayah above, all Muslim men who choose to marry more than one woman should be committed to exhibiting equality among their wives on all fronts—emotionally, financially, and physically—and refrain from prioritizing the requirements of one wife over those of the others. Since Allah (s.w.t) opposes this in Islam, you can therefore find yourself in the position of acting unjustly against your wives as the husband of numerous wives. It was reported that the Prophet (s.a.w.s) after he treated his wives with fairness, by demonstrating the idea of justice, among his wives. He would ask Allah in prayer,

> "O Allah! That is, what can I do to make justice among them? May you not blame me as regards what you possess, and I do not possess (namely the heart)."

As for the wearing of the Hijab (head and body, covering) of Muslim women, this is a commandment instructed by Allah (s.w.t) in the Qur'an, there is often a lot of discrepancy about the Qur'an using the word Khemaar (face veil and head covering).

However, Allah (s.w.t) has also instructed men to dress appropriately and to safeguard their private parts with modesty. Dress in loose-fitting clothing so as not to entice women. (Tahj) head covering and (Jalabiya) body covering as well. To guard those body parts that are appealing to the eyes of Humanity.

(Qur'an An-Nisa':4: 77-78, in part)

"The enjoyment of this worldly life is short, the life of the hereafter is much better for those who fear Allah, and rest assured that you will not be wronged equal to the fiber of a date-stone."[77] "As for death, no matter where you may be, death is going to reach you even if you are in fortified towers."[78]

Amin! Alhamdulillah! (All praise due to Allah)

Glossary

- ❖ 'Alayhis-Salaam: "May Peace be upon him."
- ❖ Allah: Al-Allah (The Creator); it is the proper name of the only Supreme Being who exists necessarily by Himself. This name comprises all the attributes of perfection.
- ❖ Akbar: Allah is All-Great.
- ❖ A.b.p.h.: Allah be pleased with her, or Allah be pleased with him.
- ❖ Adhkaar: dhikr; Remembrance of Allah
- ❖ Ahaadeeth: (hadith); sayings, deeds, and traditions of the Prophet, Hadiths,
- ❖ Ansaar: "Helpers, defenders, protectors." The Muslims of Madinah welcomed and helped the Prophet Muhammad and those who migrated from Makkah for the sake of the faith (Islam).
- ❖ 'Asr: An unlimited extent of time during which people pass away and become extinct. 'Asr is also a name used for one of the five prescribed prayers which is offered in the late afternoon.
- ❖ 'Aqeedah: Belief, Doctrine, Creed.
- ❖ Aayah: "sign"; a verse of the Qur'an.
- ❖ Birr: Righteousness, kindness, good treatment.
- ❖ Da'wah: "invitation" or "call"; calling people to Islam.
- ❖ Dunyah: This transient world, as opposed to the Hereafter.
- ❖ Dar-ul-Islam: Home of Peace…A State or Country ruled by Islamic Law (Qur'an and Sunnah), where Muslims and non-Muslims are at peace to practice their respective beliefs.

- Deen: Faith, Judgement, way of life. Islam is called 'Al-Deen.' The way of life is not a faith of rituals but a complete way of life including spiritual, social, economic, and political systems guiding private, public, national, and international issues.
- Du'aa': Supplication, private or informal prayer, which may be in Arabic or one's language,
- Fajr: Dawn; The early morning prayer, performed before sunrise.
- Fiqh: Comprehension, understanding, Jurisprudence, the understanding and application of Shari'ah.
- Fitnah: Trial, temptation, tribulation, tumult.
- Fitrah: The natural state of the man, which is Islam.
- Ghusl: Full ablution, a ritual bath.
- Hajj: Ritual pilgrimage to Makkah, from the 8th to 12th of Dhu'l-Hijjah, the 12th month of the Hijri (Muslim) calendar; one of the pillars of Islam and should be performed once in a lifetime by every Muslim who is financially and physically able to do so.
- Hijab: The Islamic dress code and related attitudes. Although the word "hijab" is often used by English-speaking Muslims to refer specifically to the head covering, it refers to the whole dress code.
- Halaal: Permitted, allowed.
- Haraam: Forbidden, prohibited.
- Isa Ibn Maryum: Jesus the Son of Mary
- Iqaamah: Call to prayer, similar to the adhaan that is given immediately before the prayer.
- 'Ishaa': The night prayer after Maghrib.

- **Imam:** Leader may refer to the person who leads others in prayers, or to the ruler or leader of an Islamic state. The word is also used as a title of respect for eminent scholars.
- **Jaahiliyah:** Ignorance. The time preceding the revelation of Islam is known as the time of ignorance. Non-Islamic.
- **Jibreel:** Gabriel, the Archangel who conveyed the revelation of the Qur'an to the Prophet.
- **Jihad:** "Struggle" or "striving"; although this word is often translated as "holy war", it has a broader meaning than warfare on the battlefield. Any act of striving to please Allah may be described as jihad,
- **Jumu'ah:** Friday, the Muslim day of gathering when men have to go to the mosque to hear the khutbah (sermon) and pray the congregational prayer. (Attendance is optional for women)
- **Kaafir:** Disbeliever, one who rejects the truth.
- **Laa ilaaha illa Allah:** There is no god but Allah. The fundamental declaration of Tawheed, the central tenet of Islam,
- **Mujahid:** The one who strives or struggles in the way of Allah (The Creator), and if required goes forth to fight for the cause of Islam.
- **Al-Masjid-al-Aqsa:** The Great Mosque in Jerusalem.
- **Al-Masjid-al-Haram:** The Sacred Mosque in Makkah which has the Ka'bah in its center.
- **Mahram:** That relationship which is declared sacred, or which is forbidden or unlawful for marriage. Examples are immediate family members, real aunts, real uncles, real nephews, and real nieces.

- **Muhajireen:** Immigrants. This term is more specifically used for those Muslims who migrated from Makkah to Madinah for the cause of Islam. They joined the Prophet leaving all their belongings behind.
- **Mushrik:** Infidel, association, idol worshipper, worshipper of anyone else besides Allah (The Creator) or the one who associates someone as a partner of Allah (The Creator) or the one who commits shirk.
- **P.B.U.H:** Peace be upon him.
- **P.B.U.T:** Peace be upon them.
- **Prophet:** A Messenger of Allah, selected by Him to pass on His message which was given through the Book of Revelations and sharia (Islamic Laws) to a Rasul. For example, the Prophet Yahyah (John) was a prophet during the time of Isa (Jesus) who was a Rasul. Therefore he (John) was required to follow the Book and Sharia given to Isa (Jesus)—peace be upon them both.
- **Qiblah:** The direction faced when praying, i.e., the direction of the Ka'ba in Makkah
- **Qiyaam al-layl:** Standing in prayer during the night.
- **Radi-Allahu 'Anhu:** "May Allah be pleased with him."
- **Radi-Allahu 'Anha:** "May Allah be pleased with her."
- **Rak'ah:** A unit or cycle of prayer. Prayer consists of two, three, or four rak'ahs.
- **Rabb:** Translated in most English translations as "Lord." Stands for: Master, Owner, Sustainer, Provider, Guardian, Sovereign, Ruler, Administrator, and Organizer.
- **Rasul:** A Prophet who is given the Book of Revelations and Sharia (Islamic Law) and is selected by Allah (The Creator) to pass on His message and be a Model for a particular nation like Ibrahim (Abraham), Lut (Lot), Musa (Moses),

Isa (Jesus) or for the whole mankind like Muhammad—peace be upon them all. "All Rasul were also Prophets, but all Prophets were not necessarily Rasul."
- <u>Salla-Allahu 'Alayhi wa Sallam:</u> "Peace and blessings of Allah be upon him". Or " May Allah honor him and grant him peace."
- <u>Subhana wa Ta'ala:</u> "The Exalted."
- <u>S.W.T.:</u> Glory be to Him, The Most High
- <u>Sahaabah:</u> The Companions of the Prophet Muhammad.
- <u>Sahih:</u> "Correct, sound, authentic." In Islamic terminology, a hadith fulfilling the conditions and criteria set by hadith scholars is termed as Sahih which is sound and most reliable.
- <u>Salaah:</u> The "formal" prayer obligatory and/or optional.
- <u>Tahajjud:</u> Voluntary prayer that is performed at night between the times of 'isha and fajr.
- <u>Taraaweeh:</u> Extra/additional prayers that are performed after 'isha during Ramadan. They are usually performed in congregation and as much of the Qur'an as possible is recited during these prayers.
- <u>Tasbeeh:</u> Saying, "Subhan-Allah", Glory be to Allah.
- <u>Tayammum:</u> It is a process of ablution when water is not available, or some medical condition prevents someone from using water. It is done with clean dust or sand, by clapping the palms of the hands on it and passing them over the hands up to elbows, repeating the same process and passing the hands over the face as if they were being washed with water.
- <u>Tajweed:</u> Correct recitation of the Qur'an, following precise rules of pronunciation and articulation.
- <u>Takbeer:</u> Saying, "Allahu Akbar." Allah is All-Great.

- Taqwwa: Piety, Taqwa involves constant awareness and remembrance of Allah, and conscious efforts to adhere to His commandments and abstain from whatever He has forbidden.
- Tawrat: Torah. It is the name of the Holy Book containing the Divine Message given to the Prophet Musa (Moses) for the guidance of Fir'aun (Pharaoh), his chiefs, and the Children of Israel.
- 'Ulama': 'Aalim. Scholars, people of knowledge.
- Ummah: Community or nation, the body of Muslims as a distinct entity. The ummah of Islam is not based on language, race, or ethnicity, but encompasses everyone who believes in Allah alone and the Prophethood of Muhammad.
- 'Umrah: The 'lesser pilgrimage," consisting of fewer rites than Hajj. 'Umrah may be performed at any time of the year.
- Wahy: Revelation, inspiration.
- Wali: to be very near to anyone, protector, friend, patron, benefactor, helper. This term is used for the friendship of Allah (The Creator) or the friendship of Shaitan (Satan). It is also used for the guardianship of a child.
- Waajib: Obligatory, compulsory.
- Witr: A prayer which has an odd number of rak'ahs. It is offered last thing at night before sleeping or following tahajjud.
- Wudoo': Partial ritual ablution is required before prayer if one has passed wind, urine, or stool.
- Yuma: A Day, a Stage, or a Time Period. It may be equivalent to one thousand years as mentioned in Surah #32 (As-Sajdah) Aayah#5, or fifty thousand years as mentioned in Surah #70 (Al-Ma'arij) Aayah #4.
- Zuhr: Midday or Noon prayer.

- <u>Zabuur:</u> Name of the Holy Book containing the Divine message given to the Prophet Dawud (David). It is also called Psalms.
- <u>Zamzam:</u> The water spring which gushed out miraculously from the feet of Prophet Isma'il (Ishmael) son of Prophet Ibrahim (Abraham) with the leave of Allah inside Masjid-al-Haram, in front of Ka'ba's door, at Makkah in Saudi Arabia? *Alhamdul Allah?*

REFERENCES

AL-BUKHARI, A. A. (2009). SAHIH BUKHARI (First ed., Vol. 1-9). (M. al-Almany, Ed., & M.M. Khan, Trans.) MEKKAH AND MADINA, MIDDLE EASTERN: KUBE Retrieved 01 26, 2016

Al-Qur'an (I-A, M. F., Trans, 15th ed.). (2019, March). Al-Qur'an The Guidance for Mankind. Al-Quran. Retrieved January 23, 2016, from https://www.al-quran.org/.

Lawal, U.A. (2015, August) Ex-husband contributed his stories growing up within an Islamic environment while maintaining his Ibadah (faith). He also contributed stories about the Prophet (s.a.w.s) through the eyes of the Shaba's (Companions).

Sunnah.com (2011, November 14). Sahih al-Bukhari Hadiths. Retrieved January 26, 2016, from https://sunnah.com/bukhari.

Qur'an Surah Al-Ma'idah 5: 56 pg.223

⁽⁵⁶⁾ "O believers! Whoever among you renounce his Deen (Islam), let them do so; soon Allah will replace them with others whom He will love, and they will love Him, who will be humble towards the believers, mighty against the unbelievers, striving hard in the way of Allah, and will have no fear of reproach from any critic. This is the grace of Allah which He bestows on whom He pleases. Allah is All-sufficient for His creatures' needs and All-knowing. ⁽⁵⁴⁾ Your real protecting friends are Allah, His Rasool, and the fellow believes—the ones who establish Salah (prayer), pay Zakah (obligatory) charity) and bow down humbly before Allah. ⁽⁵⁵⁾ Whoever makes Allah, His Rasool, and the fellow believers his protecting friends, must know that Allah's party will surely be victorious. ⁽⁵⁶⁾

Allah, Please Accept What is Written In This Book!

Alhamdul Allah! Allahu Akbar!

Made in the USA
Columbia, SC
02 November 2024

b26e392b-fdf6-4071-8658-18c0e6d0eafaR01